Routledge Revivals

Britain and the Commonwealth

First published in 1965, *Britain and the Commonwealth* provides a comprehensive account of Britain's role in the Commonwealth and of the Commonwealth's place in the modern world. The author gives sufficient historical background, deals thoroughly with the present, and on the basis of his analysis risks a forecast of the future. The institutions and systems of government of different members of the Commonwealth- very varied as they are today- are described in relation to the way in which the Commonwealth countries work together and re-act on each other.

Professor Wiseman considers the essential criteria for membership, and he does not burke the difficult issues presented by varying degrees and definitions of democracy and the rule of law in different Commonwealth members. These are the problems presented by a grouping of nations in varying stages of development, with varying cultural, religious and political backgrounds- at once the challenge to the Commonwealth today and one of the main reasons for its importance. This is an important read for students of British Politics and British history.

Britain and the Commonwealth

Herbert Victor Wiseman

Routledge
Taylor & Francis Group

First published in 1965
by George Allen & Unwin Ltd, 1965

This edition first published in 2024 by Routledge
4 Park Square, Milton Park, Abingdon, Oxon, OX14 4RN

and by Routledge
605 Third Avenue, New York, NY 10017

Routledge is an imprint of the Taylor & Francis Group, an informa business

© George Allen & Unwin Ltd, 1965

Publisher's Note
The publisher has gone to great lengths to ensure the quality of this reprint but points out that some imperfections in the original copies may be apparent.

Disclaimer
The publisher has made every effort to trace copyright holders and welcomes correspondence from those they have been unable to contact.

A Library of Congress record exists under LCCN: 0710004575

ISBN: 978-1-032-70024-3 (hbk)
ISBN: 978-1-032-70027-4 (ebk)
ISBN: 978-1-032-70025-0 (pbk)

Book DOI 10.4324/9781032700274

Britain and the Commonwealth

BY

H. VICTOR WISEMAN
M.A. (Oxon), B.Sc. (Econ.), LL.B., Ph.D.
Professor and Head of the Department of Government,
University of Exeter

London

GEORGE ALLEN & UNWIN LTD

RUSKIN HOUSE, MUSEUM STREET

FIRST PUBLISHED IN 1965
SECOND IMPRESSION 1968

PRINTED IN GREAT BRITAIN
in 10 on 11 *point Baskerville type*
BY WILLMER BROTHERS LIMITED
BIRKENHEAD

PREFACE

The immediate occasion of this book was the suggestion that a straightforward and relatively simple account of the Commonwealth and particularly of Britain's role in the Commonwealth, should be provided for overseas students who, as part of the Certificate of Proficiency in English, are expected to learn something of British Institutions and the British way of life. The intention, however, was to provide not just a descriptive handbook, but also a critical appraisal of Britain's position in the Commonwealth and of the Commonwealth's position in the world. Although the emphasis is laid on Britain's role, some account of the institutions and attitudes of other Commonwealth members is provided.

As the writing proceeded, it appeared that the book might also be of use to all those who may wish to learn a little more about the Commonwealth in a period which has seen not merely the at least temporary surmounting of a possible crisis (over Southern Rhodesia) in 1964, but a positive effort to promote further Commonwealth cooperation.

This book has been written while plans for a Commonwealth Secretariat were being drawn up, and during the discussions which led to general agreement that another Commonwealth Conference should be held in the summer of 1965. It is hoped that it may provide both background material and some ideas against which the outcome of the latest Conference may be judged.

More specifically, it may be of use to students of all kinds, ranging from those who are required to know something of the Commonwealth for British Constitution 'A' Level examinations, to college and university students who either specialize in studies of government, or are expected to include some approach to the subject in courses of 'liberal studies'.

So far as my colleagues in the field of political science are concerned, it is merely hoped that, accepting the purpose of the book, they will not find too much to criticise in it. Because of the nature of the readership which it is hoped to reach, it has not been considered necessary to provide a bibliography for further reading. Some references are, however, contained in the text.

Preface

I am grateful to my secretary, Mrs Ibbetson, for her effort to complete the typescript in very quick time, and to my students in Commonwealth Government for their unsolicited assistance in the task of being brief and simple, without, it is hoped, being inaccurate or tendentious.

February, 1965

CONTENTS

The Commonwealth as a Whole

I: FROM EMPIRE TO COMMONWEALTH

The title of this book has been deliberately chosen to emphasize that its primary focus is the place of the United Kingdom in the Commonwealth. Within a short compass it is possible to glance only briefly at the social and political systems of the other members and then primarily in order to examine to what extent they differ from the 'Westminster model' or the common pattern of institutions and ideals which are sometimes said to be important Commonwealth links. There is, of course, historical and even current justification for placing Britain at the centre, since without her there would have been no Commonwealth and without her it would probably cease to exist, certainly in its present form. But we shall examine Britain's role not only in the past and the present—transitional and changing—situation. Some attempt will be made to assess the future of the Commonwealth and this involves raising the question of how Britain's role may change and the Commonwealth become, perhaps, less Anglo-centric. Despite this emphasis upon Britain, however, our main concern is with the Commonwealth as a whole rather than with its separate parts.

One further point of explanation: we shall be concerned almost entirely with the self-governing, independent units of the Commonwealth, except in so far as its dependent parts illustrate general problems. For the status of the former, in some form or another, is sought by those latter parts which, to a greater or less extent, remain 'dependencies' of the United Kingdom.

Although the main purpose of this book is to attempt an explanation of what the 'Commonwealth' is and stands for today, there is considerable interest and perhaps some enlightenment to be derived from a brief examination of the use of the word itself. Language may have been given to us to disguise our thoughts. But there is still 'something in a name'. As long ago as 1884, Lord Rosebery described the British Empire as 'a commonwealth of nations'. Although this description was in many ways misleading, partly because there were few 'nations' within the Empire, partly because the era of expansionist imperialism, with 'the scramble for Africa' about to set the tone for all Western Nations, as well as Japan and the United States, was hardly hospital to the idea of separate nations, it did take account of the fact that the white colonies were fast growing in self-government and national consciousness. A distinction was already beginning to grow up between the relationship of Britain to India and the Crown Colonies and Protectorates on the one hand, and the 'constitutional colonies' on the other. The latter relationship (whether to those who were asserting 'colonial independence' on the one hand, or to those who were hoping for a closer 'imperial Federation' on the other) was ceasing to be 'imperial' in the sense of dominion held by Britain over unequals. In the three decades following Lord Rosebery's remarks there were many suggestions that 'British Commonwealth' might be an appropriate description for the group of units comprising Britain and the 'constitutional colonies'. Joseph Chamberlain, a great Colonial Secretary, spoke of 'sister nations' which owed 'a hearty and voluntary allegiance to a common flag, while in all other respects they enjoy the privileges and bear the burdens of independent states.' As Rudyard Kipling expressed it :

> Daughter am I in my mother's house,
> But mistress in my own.

The idea was expressed more fully by Lord Milner (another great 'pro-consul of Empire') in 1908.

> 'I often wish that when speaking of the British Empire . . . we could have two generally recognized appellations by which to distinguish the two widely different and indeed contrasted types of states of which that Empire is composed

The Commonwealth as a Whole

. . . I am thinking of the contrast between the self-govern-ing communities of European blood, such as the United Kingdom, Canada, Australia, and New Zealand, and the communities of coloured race, Asiatic, African, West Indian, or Melanesian, which though often enjoying some measure of autonomy, are in the main subject to the Government of the United Kingdom.'

He wished to speak of 'the self-governing Empire, and 'the dependent Empire.' Many, of course, were not slow to point out that in the first case 'Empire' was an unsuitable term. Nor was it enough that in 1907 the term 'Dominion' had been adopted for the white colonies and that they were distinguished from the rest by their attendance at Imperial (no longer Colonial) Conferences. The term 'Empire' was falling on evil days and not only because of its association with the German and Austrian Empires.

Yet although the term 'Commonwealth' was increasingly used in unofficial writings, it was World War I which gave it real popularity. This term, as well as 'Imperial Commonwealth', 'Britannic Commonwealth', 'Commonwealth of Nations' and 'British Commonwealth of Nations', was constantly bandied about. These different terms, however, meant different things to those who used them.

At official level, at the Imperial War Conference of 1917, Sir Robert Borden (Canada) spoke of 'an Imperial Commonwealth of United Nations' and General Smuts (South Africa) of 'the British Commonwealth'. The Conference agreed that there should be full recognition of the Dominions as 'autonomous nations of an Imperial Commonwealth', and of India as an im-portant part of the same. The term 'British Commonwealth of Nations' made its first official appearance in the Anglo-Irish Treaty of 1921 (the Irish Free State was to be given 'Dominion Status'), and was reaffirmed both in the Balfour Report of 1926 and the Statute of Westminster, 1931 (of which more below). Nevertheless, the term 'Commonwealth' continued in popular language to be applied both to the British Empire as a whole and to the privileged inner circle of self-governing members. Some spoke of 'Commonwealth and Empire'.

World War II resulted in the gradual disappearance of the

latter term, despite Mr Winston Churchill's warning that he had not become the King's First Minister in order to preside over the liquidation of the British Empire. Then, mainly for economy of language, the qualifying 'of nations' was gradually dropped. Finally, with the addition of many self-governing independent Asian and African members to the Commonwealth (with the right even to secede, as India had been assured in 1942 and as Burma did in 1947) the adjective 'British' came to be dropped.

It has been remarked that 'the simple, unadorned title, 'the 'Commonwealth' seems to be the most popular today. It is concise and comprehensive. It combines tradition with modernity. It means all things to all men.'[1] Our purpose is to try to explain something of these 'meanings', at least as understood by the members of the Commonwealth themselves.

II: THE COMMONWEALTH CONFERENCE

To the general public and to almost all of the Press, the high-water mark of the *Commonwealth in Action* is the gathering of Heads of Governments at the palace of Marlborough House, which, in 1959, the Queen placed at the disposal of the British Government for Commonwealth meetings in London. In 1964 the thirteenth such gathering, since it took the place of the Imperial Conference, included representatives of eighteen independent member-countries, although three were unable to send their Heads—India, Cyprus and Jamaica. They were Britain, Canada, Australia, New Zealand, India, Pakistan, Ceylon, Ghana, Malaysia (Malaya-Singapore-British Borneo-Sarawak), Nigeria, Cyprus, Sierra Leone, Tanzania, (Tanganyika-Zanzibar), Jamaica, Trinidad and Tobago, Uganda, Kenya (these last two represented for the first time) and Malawi (Nyasaland, whose Prime Minister attended three days after his country achieved independence). Within the year Zambia (Northern Rhodesia) and the Gambia also attained the same status.

The variety of members is shown by the fact that they came from Australasia, North America, Asia, Africa and the Caribbean. There is some interest in examining a few of their character-

[1]S. R. Mehrotra in *Journal of Commonwealth Studies*, Vol. I. No. 1.

istics. Of the fifteen Heads of States, there were a field marshal (General Ayub Khan of Pakistan) and a widow (Mrs Bandaranaike of Ceylon); a former male nurse, afterwards a barrister (Mr Margai of Sierra Leone); winners of a Nobel Peace Prize and a Lenin Peace Prize (Mr Pearson of Canada and Dr Nkrumah of Ghana); a prince, an ex-earl (Sir Alec Douglas-Home) and two other knights; three 'Prison-graduates'—those who served a term in gaol under British rule : there would have been two more if Mr Shastri (India) and President Makarios (Cyprus) had attended. Some had been politicians for many years; others were younger and less experienced in terms of time if not in intensity. Sir Robert Menzies had had fourteen unbroken years as Prime Minister of Australia, yet next to him came Dr Nkrumah who had become Prime Minister twelve years before the Conference. With a year or less as heads of their Governments was an interesting mixture—Sir Alec Douglas-Home, Mr Pearson, Mr Kenyatta (Kenya) and Mr Margai. Yet Mr Kenyatta was well over seventy, while young African leaders included Dr Nyerere (Tanzania) at forty-two and Dr Obote (Uganda) just over forty. Sir Alec Douglas-Home, Mr Pearson and Dr Williams (Trinidad) were at Oxford—the two last as Rhodes Scholars; Tunku Abdul Rahman (Malaysia) was at Cambridge; President Ayub Khan was at Sandhurst; Dr Hastings Banda (Malawi) at Edinburgh studying medicine—where he also became an elder in the Church of Scotland. Yet Mr Holyoake (New Zealand) left school at twelve to help on the family farm. Mr Kenyatta was at the London School of Economics. Both he and Sir Abubakar Tafawa Balewa (Nigeria) had been teachers, like Dr Nkrumah, whose education took in both Britain and America. Dr Nyerere and Mr Margai are Roman Catholics, President Ayab Khan and Sir Abubakar, Moslems. Mr Kenyatta and Dr Nkrumah have published 'non-fiction' books; Sir Abubakar has written a novel, the Tunku a successful play, while President Nyerere has translated *Julius Caesar* into Swahili. Privy Councillors and Companions of Honour could be found among the fifteen. Others have more revealing, if unofficial titles, like Dr Nkrumah's 'Osagyefo' (saviour), Dr Banda's 'Ngwazi' (lion) and Mr Kenyatta's 'Mzee' (the old man) : these were the 'prison graduates' present. These are but some of the characteristics which may fascinate, especially, the foreign observer of the Commonwealth scene.[1] Yet perhaps the most significant fact of all is that these representatives of every continent, race, colour, and creed, were meeting in London, were all speaking English and, as we shall see, possessed many other qualities in common.

This Commonwealth gathering included only fully independent members. Those not yet so advanced constitutionally had sent observers to the 1962 Conference because of the possible implications for them of Britain's application to join the European Economic Community. But the dependent parts of the Commonwealth were reported on by the British Prime Minister, and the other full members were greatly interested and had much to say about progress towards independence. Though we shall discuss the implications of this interest in the context of Britain's changing role in the Commonwealth, it is convenient briefly to refer here to the discussions for the information they contain about that part of the Commonwealth not represented in London.

The British Prime Minister was proud to proclaim that already more than twenty countries, with a total population of some seven hundred million had achieved sovereign independence under British guidance. Others—excluding Zambia and the Gambia—such as Basutoland, Bechuanaland, Swaziland, the Federation of South Arabia, British Guiana and Southern Rhodesia were already well on their way to such status—although in the former case Indian-Negro racial divisions and in the latter a seemingly intransigent white minority were causing delay. In addition, the Bahamas, Barbados, British Honduras and Mauritius already enjoyed a wide measure of self-government. Finally, there were about twenty other colonies and protectorates (including the 'Little Seven' islands in the British West Indies where discussions about federation were in progress) with a combined population of about five million. Three million of these were in Hong-Kong; of the rest, only two had populations of more than 100,000, while Pitcairn, in the Pacific, had only ninety!

Although there was considerable concern about British Guiana

[1] I am indebted to an article in the *Economist*, 11 July, 1964 for this information.

(where Dr Williams of Trinidad had been no more successful in bringing the two sides together than the British Colonial Secretary), Southern Rhodesia caused most anxiety. Many African (and other) leaders had come determined to oppose independence for that colony under its white-dominated constitution and with the two most prominent African leaders, Mr Nkomo and Mr Sithole, in detention. The Heads of other member-countries recognized that the authority and responsibility for leading her other colonies to independence must continue to rest with Britain. But it was clear that they hoped—and, indeed, succeeded in impressing their point of view on Britain to the extent that the latter agreed—that 'sufficiently representative institutions' were a pre-requisite of independence, and that Britain would not recognize a unilateral declaration of independence — a pledge unanimously supported by all other members. Britain further took note of the general feeling that a further conference should be held, to include, if possible, the African leaders in Southern Rhodesia, in order to discuss further constitutional reform before independence. Though there were differences of opinion on matters of detail, and no member denied Britain's ultimate responsibility, it was clear that something like a 'Commonwealth' opinion had emerged.

In the same way, in 1961, it had been a general abhorrence of apartheid, expressed most forcefully by non-white members—indeed, Tanganyika announced earlier that she would not apply for membership on achieving independence if South Africa remained in—but not by them alone, which created a situation leading to the withdrawal by South Africa of her request to remain a Commonwealth member on becoming a Republic. The Commonwealth, it has been said, increasingly justifies its existence by its multi-racial qualities alone. Certainly the agreed statement issued at the end of the 1964 Conference emphasized this point.

> The Commonwealth 'is . . . a cross-section of the world itself, and its citizens have an unparalleled opportunity to prove that, by mutual cooperation, men and women of many different races and national cultures can live in peace and work together for the common good'.

B   17

Let us look a little further at the 1964 'Commonwealth in Action' before considering the historical processes whereby the Commonwealth has become what it is. Some of the hopes expressed in the deliberations may appear somewhat over-optimistic in view of problems which we shall discuss later. But the Commonwealth is nothing unless it asserts ideals and Britain nothing within the Commonwealth unless she offers an example of striving to achieve those ideals.

Some of them are related to the problem of race-relations already mentioned. If the Commonwealth itself is 'an almost unique experiment in international cooperation among people of several races and continents', many of its members themselves are faced with the problem of co-existence of different cultures within a democratic society. Disapproval of South Africa's approach to this kind of problem led to her virtual expulsion in 1962. In 1964 the Conference emphasized that each member should strive to build a society based on equal opportunity and non-discrimination for all its people and should take the lead in the application of democratic principles to every aspect of life. How far, in particular cases, these ideals are being achieved we shall enquire later.

Problems of international relations were discussed and although the Commonwealth can have little that is distinctive to say on such matters, it is of no small importance that all its members can affirm support for such things as a test ban treaty, agreements not to place nuclear weapons in outer space and continual efforts to make further progress in general disarmament. More specifically, there was general sympathy and support for Malaysia in her confrontation with Indonesia—a notable example of ex-colonial territories refusing to accept the charge of neo-colonialism in one of their number, and for any efforts to re-establish stability in the South and South-East Asian area so frequently threatened by China. Naturally, complete support was expressed for the work of the United Nations (though later in the year some African members took a different view of events in the Congo than other Commonwealth members) and especially for the peace-keeping force in Cyprus.

The foreign observer of the Commonwealth will particularly note that disputes between members do not preclude their cooperation outside the particular field of dispute. Indeed, as the Kashmir problem, in its effect on relations between India and Pakistan, shows, Conferences provide an opportunity for fruitful informal discussions. While other members scrupulously refrain from interference in such disputes, it is notable that in 1964 the hope was expressed that Commonwealth countries might play a role of conciliation, and even use their good offices to assist in a settlement, where the other members concerned were prepared to accept mediation. In some cases, of course, joint action is impossible. Many Commonwealth countries, for example, thought that economic sanctions should be applied to end apartheid in South Africa; others doubted their efficacy—and perhaps their morality.

Economic problems inevitably loomed large and the need for trade outlets as well as loans on easier terms and continued aid was recognized. A typically Commonwealth approach, however, was seen in the desire to use methods of development which would strengthen the links between Commonwealth members and which might involve joint contributions to projects for technical development, education, administrative training, health and welfare. It had already become obvious that many members in addition to Britain might be able to make contributions of knowledge, techniques and experts. We refer later to some of the concrete results of these general discussions.

It would be tedious to examine the work of every Commonwealth Conference in the detail which it was thought useful to provide for that of 1964 in order to give a comprehensive picture of the Commonwealth at work in its most publicized form. But since such gatherings are the culminating point of more continuous contacts and exchanges of views and the opportunity for taking up, at top level, matters of outstanding importance, it is useful to look briefly at them. It must, however, be explained that since there is no formal agenda, no decisions taken except upon such outstanding constitutional matters as the admission of a newly-independent country, and no reports except a final communiqué (though in 1964 many leaders made prepared statements for the Press on such issues as Southern Rhodesia), the 'frank and uninhibited exchange of views and information'

19

which we are told takes place can be referred to only in general terms.

The Conferences of 1944 and 1946 were, of course, concerned primarily with the problems of war and the peace treaties, including preparations for a United Nations Organization. In 1949 the important decision was taken to continue India's membership of the Commonwealth as a Republic, with the King as a person (not the Crown as a legal entity) recognized as 'the symbol of the free association of its independent members and, as such, the head of the Commonwealth.' We shall say more of this historic decision when discussing the nature of the links which bind the Commonwealth together. In 1951, 1953 and 1955 international and economic matters were of most concern; in the latter year separate regional defence discussions were held by those members involved—for there is no common defence organization or policy for the Commonwealth as a whole. Pakistan notified her intention of becoming a Republic and her continuing membership was recognized. In 1956 and 1957, again, international and economic matters were to the forefront. In the former year Ceylon announced her intention to become a Republic (though this decision had still not been implemented in 1964) and in the latter, the first of the African members, Ghana, was welcomed. (In 1960 Ghana announced her intention to become a republic and her membership continued). 1960 was again a year for international and economic discussions. Malaya, endowed with her own constitutional monarchy—another innovation—attended for the first time. We have already mentioned the key conference of 1961 at which South Africa withdrew her application for continued membership as a republic. Nigeria then attended for the first time (she also later became a Republic), while Pakistan, Ghana and Cyprus (this latter at its first meeting) were represented by their Presidents. It thus became necessary to speak not of Prime Ministers' Conferences but of Gatherings of Heads of Governments. In 1962, already noted as having been concerned with the implications for the Commonwealth of Britain's possible entry into the Common Market, Sierra Leone, Tanganyika, Jamaica, and Trinidad and Tobago (these two separately independent after the break-up of the Federation of the West Indies) were welcomed for the first time. And so to 1964. . . .

During the same period the Commonwealth Economic Consultative Council, at its highest level consisting of Finance and Economic Ministers, met in London three times and in Accra, Ghana, once. Foreign Ministers met in Colombo, Ceylon, in 1950. Education Conferences were held in Oxford (1959), New Delhi (1962) and Ottawa (1964). Many other specialist conferences, to which further reference is made later, were held. Certainly the 'Commonwealth' is frequently in action at high level and, indeed, continuously in action at lower levels. But what, the foreign observer will doubtless repeat, is this Commonwealth?

III: IS THERE A COMMONWEALTH CONSTITUTION?

One thing which must be made clear is that there is no 'Constitution' of the Commonwealth; nor is the Commonwealth as a unit (unlike the British Empire) an entity in international law. Apart from the division between Monarchies (or Realms) and Republics, each Monarchy is a separate entity, the Queen being Queen of Canada, Australia etc. and advised, in each case, by the Government of the particular unit concerned; while in the case of the Republics her role as 'Head' of the Commonwealth is purely symbolical. Nor is the Commonwealth a Federation or a Confederation, although it includes some Federations, e.g. Australia, Canada, India, Nigeria, Malaysia. There are 'conventions' and 'usages' (as well as practical arrangements for consultation and cooperation which we discuss later) but nothing to prevent any member from ignoring them in any given case (though, perhaps, continuous neglect of them might be tantamount to withdrawal). There is no argument about the right of 'secession', since there is nothing, technically, to secede from. No formal treaty (apart from that which may form part of an Act of the United Kingdom Parliament granting independence) is needed to permit a member of a family who has come of age from leaving home. Though the example of Southern Rhodesia shows that if a member leaves home before achieving, in the eyes of the family, complete maturity (still more if she leaves 'unilaterally' without even the formality of a 'certificate of coming-of-age', i.e. an Independence Act), she may never be welcomed back.

More specifically, there is no top-level political decision-making machinery for the Commonwealth as a whole. (Even 'agreed decisions' which are individually accepted, for example, the decisions about South Africa, can only be implemented, so far as their practical consequences are concerned, by each individual member). Nor is there any President, Prime Minister or Cabinet for the Commonwealth (unlike, for example, the French Union or Community). The Queen, as we have said, is merely 'Head of the Commonwealth' for what the English political scientist, Bagehot, called 'dignified and ceremonial purposes' and has what he called the right 'to be consulted, to advise, to warn' only in respect of Her Government in the United Kingdom. (In the other Monarchies her role is performed by the Governor-General, though when she visits these Realms she may participate in government, e.g. by opening Parliament.) In the Republics she has not even these vestigial functions and is received by the President concerned in a purely ceremonial manner).

Certainly there is no Commonwealth Parliament, not even a Consultative Assembly like that of the Western European Union. Prime Minister Harold Wilson has suggested that eventually there might be such an assembly—as part of his general desire to make the Commonwealth more of a reality. We can be certain that if it is ever established, it will remain purely consultative, will never take formal votes, not even with safeguards for minorities as in the European Economic Community, and will never exercise control over Presidents and Prime Ministers.

There is no 'Commonwealth' Civil Service, though plans for a Commonwealth Secretariat (discussed below), if they materialize, may mark the beginning of one. There are no 'Commonwealth' Courts and the Judicial Committee of the Privy Council (again, discussed below) functions now only for very few members of the Commonwealth and not even for all the 'older' (white) Dominions.

Foreign observers of this curious entity may perhaps obtain just a little enlightenment if we briefly consider possible comparisons with other organizations. First those concerning relations between other imperial powers and their erstwhile colonies.

The Commonwealth as a Whole

The present arrangements between the U.S. and the Philippines are similar to those between Britain and *some* other Commonwealth countries. There is the system of preferential trade in some commodities and of special military arrangements like those between Britain and Malaysia. But the U.S. has this kind of relationship with one ex-colony; Britain a variety of relationships with twenty. Moreover, the U.S.-Philippines relationship is based on a treaty in which everything is set down in detail; Britain has a few treaty relationships with some ex-colonies but for the most part her relationships are informal.

The Dutch-Indonesian Union, though extremely short-lived, with its idea of two sovereign states joined together by the same constitutional monarch, and engaging in periodic consultation, clearly owed something to the Commonwealth model.

The Community, as set up under the Constitution of the Fifth French Republic, had less in common with the Commonwealth. Although it envisaged considerable autonomy for overseas territories, they were kept within close control by a variety of institutions all of which emphasized French hegemony. The *actual* relations between France and her ex-African territories now have much in common with the way in which British relations are conducted with some of her recently-independent ex-colonies. But the degree of dependence of ex-French West and, especially, Equatorial Africa upon France for finance, teachers, favoured trade and, in some cases, military assistance, makes the general relationship—in the *absence* of such machinery as exists in the Commonwealth—one of *greater* dependence on the part of the overseas territories than is the case of the Commonwealth—with much *more* elaborate machinery.

Perhaps the Commonwealth may be more readily compared with international organizations? The United Nations does not, however, offer much valid comparison. It is a forum for dealing with international political issues and a means of recruiting support when particular issues arise—as in the Congo, Israel, Cyprus (and, of course, most dramatically, Korea). It has a massive secretariat and a United Nations 'Presence' which can be manifested in a given part of the world, as well as a prominent and influential Secretary-General. The Commonwealth has none of these characteristics except that of being able to recruit support for the policies of its particular member's policies. It operates indirectly and without publicity.

There are some UN bodies with which, perhaps, closer comparison might be made. The Economic Commission for Asia and the Far East (ECAFE) for example, like the Commonwealth, emphasizes mutual discussions rather than joint action, and occasionally adopts joint projects by mutual agreement. But this body, again, has a substantial secretariat, which attempts to steer the Commission in particular directions and there is no real parallel, as we shall see, in the Commonwealth Relations Office in London (though the proposed Commonwealth Secretariat *might* eventually take such a role). Moreover, as in so many similar organizations there is often an 'atmosphere' derived from the existence of the Cold War which, despite differences of opinion between the 'committed' and the 'neutralists' does not exist in the Commonwealth.

Nor can valid comparisons be made with such alliances as NATO or SEATO. The Commonwealth has no purpose connected with military action, nor did it come into being with any particular enemy in view.

It has been suggested that the nearest comparisons with the Commonwealth are to be found in such bodies as the Organization of American States and the Nordic Council.

These are essentially consultative in their operation. But, apart from the fact that both these bodies have some sort of constitution, they are both regional in character and arise from the needs of states in a geographical area where common dangers and problems exist, where certain economic needs are shared, and where there is a broad similarity of culture. None of these features exists to any great extent in the Commonwealth, though there are regional groupings of a like nature *within* it.[1]

The Commonwealth, then, is *sui generis*. To repeat, each member remains a sovereign independent state. What difference memberships makes, (for example, Burma left the Commonwealth, India remained in; the Sudan stayed outside, Kenya stayed in—what has this meant, in fact?) we shall attempt to

[1] I am indebted, in this section, to a paper presented by Professor J. D. B. Miller to the Sixth World Congress of the International Political Science Association in Geneva, 1964.

explain later. But the legal and constitutional position is clear. If Commonwealth Conferences make recommendations which involve subsequent action by members, each member will (if it pleases) take such action in its own way and in its own time and through its own constitutional, governmental, and administrative machinery. Nor is there need for a formal "veto" to prevent action, since it is clearly understood that just as no member can be compelled to take action, neither can it be prevented from taking any action it deems in its own interest. How, then, has this curious, unprecedented group of independent sovereign states, yet with many ties that may well be stronger than any formal constitutional or treaty arrangements could provide, come into being? We are here concerned with the process whereby the British Empire, a very different entity indeed, has 'evolved' into the Commonwealth.

IV: THE DURHAM REPORT, DOMINION STATUS, AND INDEPENDENCE

'There could have been no Commonwealth had there not been a British Empire. Equally there could have been no Commonwealth but for the negation, withdrawal and transformation of British imperialism.' So writes Mr Patrick Gordon Walker in his book *The Commonwealth*. When Britain's 'First Empire' came to an end with the loss of the American Colonies, leaving little but India, some West Indian possessions and a few scattered outposts, Britain pursued two policies. One was to extend her influence in India and the Far East, and later in Africa (though with some reluctance and sometimes even retreat). The other was to take any measures deemed necessary to forestall any repetition of the American revolution, including the abandonment of policies which restricted the growth of self-government. Inevitably, there developed a distinction between colonies of settlement and colonies of conquest and administration. British policy involved the treatment of every colony as an entity with its own local government which involved at least some degree of influence by local opinion. This framework encouraged the growing force of nationalism. But it also encouraged the development

25

of at least the outward forms of parliamentary democracy and the rule of law and, with the spread of the English language, the reading of the same books and the discussion of similar ideas. As a result, to quote Mr Gordon Walker again, 'the creation of a Commonwealth . . . was not by any means an exclusively British achievement . . . The British idea of the nation, like that of the other members, was itself shaped by the process of Commonwealth evolution.'

The 'Commonwealth' derives its principal characteristics from the relationship of Britain with a particular group of colonies, those settled by white men and which were the first to become 'self-governing'. But they achieved their nationhood within, not outside, the Empire. Later, the Asian and African nations were undoubtedly influenced in their decision to continue in the Commonwealth by the fact that it contained a number of powerful and indubitably sovereign nations. Canada led the way and set the pattern for the evolution of parliamentary democratic nations out of the colonies of settlement. Unrest and rebellion led to the famous Durham Report of 1839. For Canada, eventually, this meant the introduction of responsible Cabinet Government and an attempt to separate local Canadian affairs from imperial affairs. In 1867 the Dominion of Canada was born, first as a federation of Ontario and Quebec, Nova Scotia and New Brunswick. Manitoba was added in 1870, British Columbia in 1871, Prince Edward Island in 1873, Saskatchewan and Alberta in 1905 and Newfoundland in 1959.

Meanwhile settlements in Australasia were providing the basis of further self-governing colonies to be based on the principles of the Durham Report. New South Wales achieved internal self-government in 1853, Tasmania and Victoria in 1855, South Australia in 1858, Queensland in 1859 and Western Australia in 1890. In 1900 these six states formed the Federal Commonwealth of Australia. New Zealand became a self-governing colony on her own in 1855 and achieved 'Dominion Status' in 1907.

In South Africa a similar process began with the British Colonies. In 1872 Cape Colony and in 1893 Natal became self-governing. After the South African war the Boer Republics of the Transvaal and the Orange Free State were given parliamentary institutions and internal self-government. In 1909 all four units formed the Union of South Africa which, before its departure from the Commonwealth in 1962, played a considerable part in the evolution of 'Dominion status' and the Commonwealth.

There is no space to develop even a brief history of the evolution of India and the Crown Colonies and other dependencies into independent self-governing nations. With our focus of attention the Commonwealth as a whole, we must turn to the changing relationships between Britain and the self-governing Dominions. By the time other British dependencies were ready for self-government these relationships had evolved in such a way as to make it possible for new members to remain within the Commonwealth without the slightest derogation to their independent status.

For some considerable time the self-governing colonies, although entirely free (subject to the very remote possibility of a 'veto' from London) in their internal affairs, had no independent status in external affairs (with some exceptions so far as trading policy was concerned). For the purpose of international law they were parts of the British Empire (which also included overseas possessions in the Caribbean, India, South-East Asia and Africa) and which was regarded as part of the 'unitary' United Kingdom. Each absorbed people and capital from Britain; each had problems of its relations with neighbouring countries in dealing with which Britain had special responsibilities. Yet, while each was subordinate to Britain and could not pursue an independent foreign policy, each had its own particular problems (for example, Canada vis-à-vis the United States, Australia vis-à-vis developments in the Far East) and its own views of world problems which it strove to impress upon the British Government. Consultations took place at successive Colonial Conferences.

The first of these was held in 1887 on the occasion of Queen Victoria's Golden Jubilee, though this was also attended by representatives of India and the Crown Colonies, i.e. those which were not self-governing even in internal affairs. The Colonial Conferences of 1897 and 1902 were confined to the 'self-governing colonies' and were primarily concerned with political and commercial relations and naval and military defence. At the last of these Conferences in 1907 a decision was taken that future

Britain and the Commonwealth

Conferences between the 'Dominions' and Britain should be called Imperial Conferences. Mr Gordon Walker writes :—

> 'If a single year is sought as the birth-date of the Commonwealth, 1907 will serve better than any other. In that year the term 'Dominion' was adopted by general agreement to describe the self-governing countries of the Commonwealth : and the "Colonial Conference" was rechristened "Imperial Conference" to signify that these countries were no longer to be regarded, or at least described as Colonies.'

The first 'Imperial' Conference, in 1911, was followed by a series of such meetings between Prime Ministers of the Dominions with the British Prime Minister in the Chair; each was purely advisory and consultative, with no executive or legislative authority; nor were their resolutions in any way binding on participants. Although during World War I no Imperial Conference as such was held, consultations frequently took place with visiting Prime Ministers and other Ministers who were invited to attend meetings of the British War Cabinet. In 1917 an Imperial War Cabinet was created and this body, which included United Kingdom and Dominion Ministers, met for several months in 1917 and 1918. At the same time Imperial War Conferences were held to consider post-war problems. That of 1917 resolved that India (*not* a Dominion) should be represented at all such Conferences in the future. After a Conference of Prime Ministers and representatives of Britain, the Dominions, and India in 1921, mainly on questions of foreign policy and defence, the series of Imperial Conferences proper was resumed in 1923. Further such Conferences were held in 1926, 1930 and 1937. All were held in London; the British Prime Minister presided; they were primarily for Prime Ministers of the Dominions (though India was represented); they were for discussion rather than decision—except on certain constitutional matters for the understanding of which we must go back a little.

Throughout the developments described above the original 'Durham' distinction between 'internal' and 'imperial' matters remained. It was reflected in the status of the Governor-General, the King's representative in the Dominions. Appointed by the

28

Crown on the advice of United Kingdom Ministers, he reported to them and was ultimately answerable to them. He might 'reserve' legislation duly passed by Dominion Parliaments 'for the signification of His Majesty's pleasure', i.e. for the decision of the British Government, and some measures he was *instructed* to reserve. Such powers of reservation were, however, seldom used, Moreover, the United Kingdom Parliament had unlimited powers to legislate for all Commonwealth countries and colonial laws 'repugnant' to United Kingdom legislation applying to the colony were invalid. The British Government could also 'disallow' colonial legislation, though the power was not used in New Zealand after 1867, in Canada after 1873, and never in Australia or South Africa. In fact, 'imperial' matters generally involved only foreign relations, overseas trade (with great freedom for the Dominions here, however, even to the extent of placing tariffs on British goods), and 'the constitution of the form of government'.

World War I had a tremendous impact upon these last remaining limitations on Dominion autonomy. But by consultation and delegation even in the 'imperial' spheres the 'unity of action' of the Empire had been slowly eroded over the years. It is now customary to regard this process as inevitable, and perhaps it was. We must nevertheless look briefly at attempts to counter it before describing its ultimate end. In the 1870's there was a movement to create federal organs to take over the exercise of authority in the imperial sphere and in 1886 the Imperial Federation League began a decade of propaganda in favour of federation as the only alternative to disintegration. Defence and 'imperial preference' (or a customs union) were of principal concern. The movement appealed particularly to Australia and New Zealand and to British communities in South Africa and Canada. But it was Canada, with her French Canadians (and, later, South Africa with her Afrikaner population) which finally destroyed the notion of federation. Neither wanted a 'British' Commonwealth. Canada opposed the idea of contributions paid for imperial defence as early as 1907, though both she and Australia accepted assistance with the establishment of Dominion fleets which would work with the Royal Navy. A New Zealand proposal in 1911 for an elected Imperial Council of Defence was turned down by Canada and South Africa because it implied a centralized and federalized Commonwealth, and by the British Prime Minister because it would 'destroy the authority of the United Kingdom'. Proposals for a permanent commission in London to carry out business in the intervals between Imperial Conferences were turned down in 1905 and 1907, largely owing to Canadian opposition.

But although every attempt to create 'Commonwealth' institutions foundered on the rock of national independence, the whole of the Empire, including the Dominions, was committed by Britain's declaration of war in 1914. Yet the war itself fostered the national aspirations of the Dominions by the very fact of their contribution to the war effort and these aspirations were still further developed immediately afterwards. At the peace conferences the Dominions were represented in the main negotiations as part of the British Empire delegation, but also separately where their own particular interests were involved. In the signatures to the Treaty of Versailles, the United Kingdom was not separately listed but signed for the 'British Empire'; all the Dominions signed on their own behalf. Each Commonwealth Parliament insisted on separately ratifying the Treaty. Similarly, in the League of Nations, the United Kingdom represented the British Empire whilst the Dominions sat and voted separately. These precedents were subsequently followed at other international conferences and for other treaties. Meanwhile Canada (and the Irish Free State, which became a Dominion in 1922) established separate diplomatic representation in Washington. At the Imperial Conference of 1923 it was agreed (as so often, *after* the event) that each Dominion had the right to negotiate and sign treaties and, if it so wished, to seek the approval of its own Parliament. On the other hand it was also declared to be 'desirable' that each member should give due consideration to the interests of the other members and to those of the Empire as a whole.

Meanwhile, Canada and South Africa had begun to press at the 1921 Conference for a new definition of Dominion rights, and while Australia was opposed to a formal and theoretical definition of the Commonwealth she was often in favour of practical changes which undermined its established concept. At the Imperial Conference of 1926, two important steps were taken. Firstly, it was laid down that a Governor-General was in all respects to occupy the same position in relation to a Dominion Government as that of the King to the Government of Great Britain. He was not to be the latter's agent in the Dominions and the recognized official channel of communication should be between Government and Government direct. Thus the King became Head of State of each separate Commonwealth nation. Secondly, the famous Balfour Declaration was adopted. The Dominions were defined as 'autonomous communities within the British Empire, in no way subordinate one to the other in any aspect of their domestic or external affairs . . . ' The Durham distinction between 'local' and 'imperial' was at last formally removed. They were, however, 'united by a common allegiance to the Crown, and freely associated as members of the British Commonwealth of Nations.' In fact, all that 'common allegiance' meant was that *each* of the King's realms, including the United Kingdom, owed a separate, distinct, and equal allegiance to the King in respect of its own territory but that it was one and the same King to which each of his realms owed its separate territorial allegiance. It must again be emphasized that this was quite different from a 'common allegiance' denoting that the Crown was the source of authority in matters of imperial concern. 'In theory the Crown could be advised in regard to the imperial sphere by a collective imperial cabinet,' but, says Mr Gordon Walker, 'in practice . . . the Crown acted in matters of imperial concern on the advice of United Kingdom Ministers.'

Between the Imperial Conferences of 1926 and 1930, detailed study was devoted to the legal implications of the Balfour formula. In the meantime, some Dominions proceeded to establish separate diplomatic representation in countries other than the United States. Australia insisted upon the selection of an Australian as Governor-General, whose appointment was, for the first time, countersigned by the Prime Minister of the Dominion and not by the United Kingdom Prime Minister. But the main result of the work done between 1926 and 1930 was the Statute of Westminster, 1931.

This removed the legal supremacy of the British Parliament. All restrictions on Dominion legislation, including the doctrine of 'repugnancy' (see above p. 29), were removed, subject to certain agreed exceptions. Once more we quote Mr Gordon Walker.

'. . . The embodiment of the Balfour formula in the Statute of Westminster formed a major landmark in the evolution of the Commonwealth. It greatly clarified the role of the Crown in the Commonwealth. Although it confused together the two roles of the Crown, it clearly implied for the first time that there were two roles. This facilitated the solution of very complex problems about the Crown that arose when India became a republic . . . The ultimate significance of the 1926-31 process was that it showed that the principle of equality of nations was inseparable from the principle of equality of race. The main motive force behind the Balfour formula and the Statute of Westminster was the need of Canada and South Africa to unite their two constituent white races within nations that could also be members of the Commonwealth. The declaration of the equal rights of Canada and South Africa in the Commonwealth was simultaneously the declaration of equality of Afrikaners and French-speaking Canadians with the British in the Commonwealth. It was thereby made possible for the Commonwealth in due course to embrace proud nations and proud races in Asia and Africa'.

In the next ten years or so even 'Dominion status' had to give way to the notion of 'Members of the Commonwealth'. Equality of status was no longer just to ensure internal unity or prestige, but to enable members to play the actual role in the world of which they were becoming capable in their own right. World War II set the seal upon all this. Unlike 1914, the United Kingdom's declaration of war in 1939, although accepted by Australia and New Zealand as committing them (though their Parliaments passed motions to approve and confirm the declaration, and the countries concerned alone decided upon the nature and degree of their actual participation), did not involve South Africa or Canada. The former declared war only after the replacement of General Hertzog by General Smuts; the latter declared war three days later after debate in Parliament. India's involvement without consultation was one factor which intensified her demand for full 'Dominion status'.

Mr Gordon Walker's account, which we have largely followed in this section has been criticized by Professor M.S. Rajan in his *Post War Transformation of the Commonwealth,* on the grounds that it does less than justice to the significance of India's decision to remain within the Commonwealth and her subsequent acceptance when she became a Republic. We may briefly examine his arguments for the light they throw on the new post-World War II Commonwealth. India's decision, Professor Rajan asserts 'finally disposed of any lingering doubts about the compatibility of nationalism and national independence and dignity with Commonwealth membership . . . and this made way for further accessions to Commonwealth membership by other Asian-African nations on attaining independence'. By the accession of India, Pakistan and Ceylon the Commonwealth became a multi-racial, multi-cultural and multi-lingual Commonwealth. This paved the way for further African members as they became independent. Conversely, this development underlined the fact that racial and cultural ties were *not* the essential basis of the Commonwealth. In addition, it involved the implicit acceptance of racial equality as an additional and new obligation of membership and led to the eventual withdrawal of South Africa in 1961.

Further, Professor Rajan argues that the change of attitude of Indian nationalists, still with 'fresh and bitter memories of the cruelties, indignities and humiliations suffered by the country as a whole as well as individual Indians under British rule', towards Britain—helped, too, by a reciprocal change in the attitude of the White Dominions and Britain herself—impressed other nationalist movements. 'It must have . . . impressed on them that such a transformation in the relations between the imperial power and colonial peoples was only possible within the framework of the then British Commonwealth of Nations, and that therefore it was as much in the interests of their own newly-independent countries as those of the still-dependent territories of the world to foster such a unique association of nations.' Beyond the legal and constitutional developments there was a 'complete psychological, emotional, and sentimental change of attitude'.

Finally, the nationalist revulsion against all things British came to be modified after the achievement of independence. The British cultural heritage of the English language, laws and legal institutions, the educational system, economic and commercial organization and many other things, was not completely rejected. Its best features were retained, modified to suit the needs of each individual country. Nor were these institutions retained simply because of their merits. 'They were retained . . . partly because they were "links of affinity" with the rest of the Commonwealth, and as such gave us a sense of belonging to a wider and friendly community of nations'.

In general, 'the development of multilateral relationships among members of the Commonwealth—in place of the earlier merely bilateral relationships between each member and Great Britain—is a post-war phenomenon largely developed by the new Asian-African members'. In so far as the Commonwealth has become very largely a purely functional association based on friendship and common interest, this development was implicit in inter-Commonwealth relationships before 1947. Since then, this association, however, has come to embrace far more than a group of predominantly white nations. 'The Commonwealth is not simply another name for the old British Empire and . . . it does not in fact constitute a block of nations. To that extent the Commonwealth has become more acceptable, and thereby influential in world affairs'. But this is to anticipate our later consideration of the role of the Commonwealth.

V : FORMAL AND INFORMAL COMMONWEALTH TIES

First, however, let us re-examine this historical process of development from an analytical point of view. We have seen that the four 'older Dominions', Canada, Australia, New Zealand and South Africa, were recognized as completely independent by the Balfour Declaration of 1926 and the Statute of Westminster, 1931. What, then, were the links remaining between them and the United Kingdom?

Firstly, there was their free association as equal members of the Commonwealth.

Secondly, there was common allegiance to the British Crown and a common British nationality.

Thirdly, there was the factor of a common British stock, although the assertion of this as a bond of unity always tended to overlook the significance of the large Afrikaner (and even larger indigenous) population of South Africa and the large and increasingly self-conscious French community in Canada (Quebec), not to mention the Maoris of New Zealand and other smaller groups of non-British Europeans and Asians in all the countries concerned.

Fourthly, there was the common possession of British institutions (not in the least affected by the existence of Federal Constitutions in Australia and Canada). Executive, legislative and judicial functions followed the United Kingdom model; the Government was responsible to Parliament, the judges were independent; the rule of law prevailed (with, however, significant exceptions in relation to the treatment of 'indigenous' populations).

Fifthly, the final court of appeal from the superior courts of all four Dominions was the Judicial Committee of the Privy Council sitting in London and consisting primarily of the same Law Lords as constituted the House of Lords as the ultimate court of appeal in the United Kingdom.

Finally, there were a number of loose links between all the members, which could, of course, be broken at any time by any member acting unilaterally, but which all the members regarded as advantageous to themselves. There were, for example, reciprocal trading and economic advantages and agreements arrived at rather more informally than through treaties. Representatives in member capitals were High Commissioners with rather more intimate contacts with the Governments concerned than Ambassadors enjoyed. There were, as we have seen, the regular Prime Ministers' Conferences. Consultation at a number of levels was continuous and provided perhaps the most significant link of all. Among other results were the defence arrangements which produced valuable results in both World Wars.

Since 1947 sixteen new members have been admitted to the Commonwealth; the term Dominion has ceased to be used;

'British' is now omitted from the title of the association. What has happened to the six links described above?

Certainly 'free association' remains, since the Commonwealth continues to exist. But 'common allegiance' has gone with the acceptance of Republics as full members, while Malaysia has its own constitutional monarch and the President of Uganda is none other than the Kabaka (King) of Buganda. In all these countries the Queen is merely the 'Head of the Commonwealth'—a description incorporated into the new royal style and titles in 1953—and has no constitutional functions to perform as she has in her 'realms', whether personal or through a Governor-General. The precedent of India, with the Queen as a purely symbolical link, has been followed elsewhere. But even those members who retain the Queen as formal Head of State are separate monarchies—the Queen is Queen of Canada 'separately' from her role as Queen of the United Kingdom—and they appoint, for example, their own ambassadors. Nor is there any 'common nationality' remaining. Each member country now defines by law its own citizens and although, in general, it distinguishes between the citizens of the Commonwealth countries and aliens, it imposes certain restrictions on the former, and, in some cases, the distinction is of small importance. Although the citizens of each Commonwealth country (as defined by its own laws) are also recognized by Britain (and by some other Commonwealth countries) as 'British subjects' or 'Commonwealth citizens', the advantage of this, again, is ceasing to be obvious. Even Britain herself no longer freely admits 'Commonwealth citizens' since the Commonwealth Immigrants Act of 1962 though they still have certain advantages over aliens, e.g. they can go on the Register of Voters after the qualifying period of residence without becoming 'naturalized' as is the case with aliens'.[1]

To turn to our third criterion (above p. 35), since we have already emphasized the 'multi-racial' nature of the Common-

---

[1]To complete the picture it may be mentioned that those who are not citizens of an independent member are called 'citizens of the United Kingdom and Colonies': this is not to be confused with 'British subject' or 'Commonwealth citizen' as defined above. The latter term, of course, includes the former.

wealth as perhaps its most significant feature, clearly the 'myth' of a common British stock is no longer of any significance.

What of the common possession of British institutions? We shall examine this in more detail in our section on the constitutions of the Commonwealth countries. But clearly, even in the 'Monarchies' (still more in the Republics) the 'Westminster model' has in many cases been almost completely replaced, while in others it is working under very different political and social conditions from those which prevail in the country of origin. A Central Office of Information pamphlet published in 1961 referred only to 'deviations' in Pakistan, Ghana, and Cyprus. Since then some member countries have as a matter of deliberate policy or as a reaction to political, economic and social problems, become virtually one-party states. Many have modified in practice certain traditional aspects of the rule of law, including the independence of the judges. On the other hand, in other countries, parliamentary government, albeit with modifications, as in India; or with serious weakness, as in Ceylon; or with potential threats, as in Nigeria in 1964; or with apparent success, as in Malaysia; has persisted. Even in those members where such apparently promising signs do not appear to exist, it is usually asserted that the 'ultimate aim' is to establish democracy more firmly and it can certainly not be ruled out as impossible of achievement. But it is significant that apologists now increasingly attempt to prove the existence of democracy even, for example, in one-party states.

So far as the appeal to the Judicial Committee of the Privy Council is concerned, it exists now only in Australia, New Zealand, Ceylon, the Federation of Malaysia (by special arrangement), Sierra Leone, the Gambia, Jamaica, Trinidad and Tobago, Uganda and Malawi—but in none of the Republics. To avoid the impression that this is a feature due only to 'non-British' influence, it must be emphasized that Canada finally abolished the right of appeal in 1949. Nor is it likely that any proposals for a new Commonwealth Court of Appeal will be adopted.

Only the final group of informal links appears, then, as strong and significant as ever, and to furnish evidence of the continued desire for 'free association'. Indeed, they are in many ways absolutely, as well as relatively, of increasing importance.

Britain and the Commonwealth

VI: THE MEANING OF COMMONWEALTH MEMBERSHIP

If therefore, almost everything which constituted the bonds between the four 'older Dominions' and Britain has disappeared what is left? Professor Miller has said that he can discern only three rules. First, the initial membership does not become automatic upon a former British Colony's becoming independent, but must be requested of the existing members. Secondly, the Queen must be recognized as the symbol of free association. Thirdly, when a member changes from monarchial to republican status, the fact must be notified to the other members. Naturally, willingness to cooperate is implicit in the request for admission. It may, perhaps, be added, as a consequence of the withdrawal of South Africa (and the debate on Southern Rhodesia) that no country governed by an unrepresentative white minority will be admitted.

Two other conditions, suggested at an unofficial Commonwealth Relations Conference in Lahore in 1954—that a member must have a firmly established parliamentary system and sufficient size and resources to support the responsibilities of a sovereign state—are clearly no longer applicable. On the first, Professor Nicholas Mansergh wrote to *The Times* in 1956 that there was little to be gained, and much might be lost in the circumstances of contemporary Asia (one could add Africa), by seeking to impose an exacting standard in respect of government. On the second, a very large number of sovereign states, outside as well as inside the Commonwealth, would fail to qualify. Nor has the suggestion that a 'two-tier' Commonwealth with different levels of responsibility and participation met with any approval except from such people as Sir Roy Welensky who has argued that African states contributing so small an amount to world progress ought not to have a say in the Commonwealth completely out of proportion with their contribution in wealth, people, or power. Even the idea that members should speak 'a common political language' has grown somewhat thin, although it may, at least, be doubtful whether a pro-Communist state would be readily admitted.

So far, with the exception of Cyprus, which achieved independence outside the Commonwealth in 1960 but was admitted to membership in the following year, all members have entered the Commonwealth directly from 'the Empire'. The 'older Dominions' did so gradually, the process culminating in the Balfour Declaration, 1926, and the Statute of Westminster, 1931. For the newer members there have been two stages (often rapidly passed) : first, the granting of independence by the United Kingdom (expressed in an Independence Act of the United Kingdom Parliament); second, a request by the newly-independent member (through the United Kingdom) to existing members for admission to the Commonwealth. However, we may note that other members besides Britain now feel entitled at least to express an opinion about the granting of independence—witness the declaration by Tanganyika and Uganda in 1963 in favour of early independence for Kenya and also the debate on Southern Rhodesia in 1964. There is no doubt that at the second stage all voices must be heard. This follows from 'equality of status'. Not that unanimity is required, though a dissenting minority might, of course, refuse to recognize the status of the new member, or even 'secede'.

It appears, so far, that when a member renounces allegiance to the Crown by becoming a Republic (or a separate Monarchy) it must have obtained *prior* consent from other members to continue its membership. It was this rule which indirectly led to South Africa's leaving the Commonwealth. Subsequent notifications by Pakistan, Ghana and others apparently provoked little or no discussion. Zambia was the first to enter immediately as a Republic without the intervening stage of independent status as a separate monarchy. Refusal to accept South Africa's application without conditions, however, which led to the latter's withdrawal, was clearly not due to its proposed new status as a Republic. Apartheid was the issue. Professor S.A. de Smith in his *New Commonwealth and its Constitutions* suggested that if membership is to be refused for such specific reasons, it might be better that they should be openly and avowedly expressed. The question of becoming a Republic would then be recognized as purely formal and perhaps require only 'information' to be given, not an application for continued membership.

So far as discontinuance of membership is concerned, it is

clear that ceasing to be an independent state or to recognize the Queen as Head of the Commonwealth, would involve cessation of membership. Members may join other associations but not become completely merged in another state whether unitary or federal. The Ghana-Guinea Union did not last long enough for this proposition to be tested in practice. Had Britain become a member of the European Ecomomic Community and had its political institutions developed as envisaged by the Treaty of Rome and subsequent discussions, the Commonwealth might have survived but it would certainly have become an entirely different kind of association. It is difficult to see, for example, what place there would have been for a 'Head of the Commonwealth'. The fanciful may wish to consider the possibility that Britain might have been 'expelled' from the Commonwealth! In fact, whether or not it is possible to expel a member must remain doubtful, though all other members might in practice deny it the facilities and privileges of membership. But, as has been rightly said, 'members decide what they want to do, and then bring the rules up-to-date'.

Once again our foreign observer is likely to enquire whether an organization which apparently has rules concerning only achieving, retaining, and relinquishing membership has any real purpose. Why is membership sought and retained? There must be objects and obligations! A typically English way of replying to such questions is to use such metaphors as family, club, college meeting, lodge. But, as has been asked, does this merely disguise the fact that 'the Emperor has no clothes'?

Mr Gordon Walker has described the Commonwealth as a 'professional, technical, parliamentary, legal, and scientific community—linked together by physical and human communication and by the maintenance of common standards, a true cultural community on a scale not seen since the Middle Ages'. John Strachey, author of *The End of Empire,* in language which would certainly be almost incomprehensible to anyone not brought up in the English tradition, once said that 'to know a no-ball from the googly and a point of order from a supplementary question is genuinely to have something in common'. Every member certainly has historical links with Britain and in the 'older Dominions' there is a powerful sense of affinity with Britain and with one another—loyalty to a common Crown (though in French-speaking Canada this loyalty appeared to have worn very thin during the Queen's tour in 1964); a somewhat ambivalent affection for what some people call the old country (though the irony of this may be illustrated by the contrast between the way in which, for example, West Indians used frequently to demand 'home" i.e. United Kingdom leave, and the way in which even Australians of British origin refer scathingly to English 'pommies'!); memories of comradeship in two world wars; and wide-spread feeling that they are all essentially one people (though clearly the Afrikaners of South Africa were excluded from this even when their country was a member); a broad measure of agreement as to the appropriate forms and ends of government. Mr Gordon Walker, indeed, argues that many of these ties of 'affinity' apply as much to the new members, though this is probably true rather of the English-educated élite who do not necessarily retain power or even predominant influence after independence and are certainly in a small minority.

But there are clearly also ties of self-interest. Britain's own stature and influence in the world would certainly be smaller if the Commonwealth did not exist; this we discuss later with specific reference to the role of the United Kingdom. Other members clearly have some interest in membership since even the most fervent exponent of ties of 'affinity' would not argue that these alone would produce a request for membership, still less a continuance of it in the absence of other advantages. An application when about to become independent will, of course, bring with it help in the form of gifts and loans—the 'golden handshake'. Indeed, offers may be increased by persuasive argument even by the smallest member, as the experience of Trinidad and Malawi shows. There is increased possibility of recruiting administrators, technical advisers, teachers, as well as receiving valuable capital assistance. The recruited 'expatriates', although increasingly supplemented from elsewhere, speak English and, up to a point at least, understand the attitude and the needs of the countries in which they serve. African members have the advantage of technical aid under the Special Commonwealth African Assistance Plan. All members, though perhaps with decreasing significance, have preferential access to the British market and to British capital.

Yet, again, in view of the increasing possibilities of material assistance from other sources (it is significant, for example, that some Commonwealth members are prepared to consider Associate Membership of the European Common Market), it would appear that there are yet other advantages to be derived from Commonwealth membership. There is the friendly, often intimate cooperation and association with a group of influential countries in many continents. Members will not be diplomatically isolated; for example there is a 'Commonwealth Group' at the United Nations—though it is certainly not always united in its attitudes to problems which arise and there is the counter-attraction of the 'Afro-Asian bloc'.

Again, there is the stream of diplomatic information that issues from the Commonwealth Relations Office in London and in all discussions there is at least the certainty that all views will be listened to sympathetically and taken into account, even though differences of opinion remain. There will be immediate aid in time of trouble—witness the case of India on the occasion of the Chinese invasion (though Pakistan and Ghana were, to say the least, lukewarm, Britain, Australia and Canada responded at once); also Tanganyika, Uganda and Kenya on the occasion of the army mutinies.

Nor must one minimize the 'multitude of unofficial links of every kind'. These range from cricket test matches and Commonwealth Games to associations of Commonwealth parliamentarians, lawyers, and journalists.

But one must speak with more hesitation than some official publications about 'common ideals' as opposed to 'convergent interests'. Common beliefs in international peace and stability, racial non-discrimination, prosperity, expanding international trade, investment in developing countries, are shown by many outside the Commonwealth and to realize most of them cooperation and assistance from outside the Commonwealth is clearly essential. The ending of colonization, the abolition of foreign military bases, the destruction of apartheid, the maintenance of parliamentary democracy and the rule of law—on all these there are differences of emphasis, differences in commitment,

42

and, above all, differences in regard to what, if any, action might be taken to deal with such issues or foster such causes.

Even the 'general understandings' which are said to constitute the real basis of Commonwealth relations are not always fully observed. To what extent, for example, is it true that there is 'an obligation to inform or consult, as may be appropriate, all other members on any projected action that might affect their interest, especially in relation to foreign affairs'? Britain, perhaps, normally accepts this obligation, though she certainly did not comply with it before going into Suez. On this occasion there was a real threat to the existence of the Commonwealth, and the division was not between old and new members—Canada was as condemnatory as India. Other members complained of 'inadequate' consultation about the consequences of Britain's possible entry into the Common Market. Yet although they themselves may generally consult with Britain, this is not so with regard to their fellow-members. In so far as 'conventions' exist, it is clear that those which insist upon national sovereignty are more clearly formulated and best observed; those which might limit freedom of action are most dubious and most likely to be ignored when self-interest demands.

As for closer constitutional links, even in the days of 'Empire', as we have seen, suggestions for an imperial federation or an imperial cabinet, or even for an arbitration tribunal, foundered on the rocks of Dominion nationalism. They are less likely than ever now to be established—with the one possible exception of a Commonwealth Secretariat, of which more below. Even in more material fields it will be shown later that neither the Sterling Area nor Commonwealth Preference is coterminous with the Commonwealth. To what extent existing ties depend on the central role of Britain is discussed below.

VII : THE MACHINERY OF CONSULTATION AND CO-OPERATION

First, however, we must examine in detail the machinery of Commonwealth consultation and cooperation. For although top-level conferences 'make the news' in a big way, especially if controversial issues such as apartheid in South Africa, Britain's application to join the Common Market, or the problem of Southern Rhodesia, are discussed, far more is achieved in actual fact and in laying the foundations for future action than is revealed in the communiqués issued. Moreover, there is much truth in the assertion that Commonwealth cooperation is 'most effective in the least politically sensitive areas of public activity'. So we turn to a more detailed consideration of the machinery of consultation and cooperation.

First, there are the activities of the High Commissioners and their advisers on such subjects as trade, the services, finance, labour, and aviation. Although these at first provided links between Britain and other members, the latter now increasingly appoint such representatives in each others' capitals. Most written communications between Commonwealth Governments are routed through the High Commissioners. This exchange of written information is supplemented by personal contact between the High Commissioners and their staffs and the Governments of the member countries in which they are posted. In London, the Commonwealth High Commissioners meet periodically with the Secretary of State for Commonwealth Relations and a Foreign Office Minister. They may arrange *ad hoc* meetings with these Ministers and, indeed, with any other Ministers concerned with the particular business under consideration. Freedom of consultation at all levels is the keynote of the activities of these continually operating links between Commonwealth members.

The Commonwealth Relations Office deserves special consideration. As early as 1907 there was a special Dominions Division of the Colonial Office and in 1925 a post of Secretary of State for Dominion Affairs was created and a Dominions Office took over from the Colonial Office business connected with the self-governing Dominions and one or two other areas, although until 1930 there was only one Minister. (In 1964 the Conservative Government decided once more permanently to merge the two departments—there had been only one Secretary of State from 1962; but this decision was reversed by the Labour Government which included two separate Secretaries of State and two distinct Departments.) In 1947 the title Dominions Office was changed to Commonwealth Relations Office. Its ministerial head is always included in the British Cabinet and his Office is the main channel through which information is received from, and communicated to, the British High Commissioners in the other Commonwealth countries. Something like thirty-five to forty thousand telegrams a year go out from the Commonwealth Relations Office on every possible subject of mutual interest—foreign affairs, defence co-operation, economic matters, even British domestic issues likely to be of interest to the other members. On foreign policy the Office works in close association with the Foreign Office. Indeed, the Office now conducts a service not unlike that of the Foreign Office except that its work is concerned with the nations of the Commonwealth and not with foreign countries. It must be emphasized that this work is related to sovereign states and is essentially diplomatic. Unlike the Colonial Office, it is not an administrative department and once its negotiations on a particular subject are completed it has no responsibility for any subsequent detailed administrative measures that may be necessary.

There has been a suggestion that the Commonwealth Relations and Foreign Offices might be merged. The Plowden Committee, whose recommendation that the two *services* (i.e. staff at home and overseas) should be amalgamated in a new Diplomatic Service was accepted and is now being implemented, also recommended as a long term project that the Ministries themselves should be amalgamated, though for reasons which we note later, not at present. Others take the view that although no other Commonwealth country has a separate Commonwealth Ministry (some have separate sections in the Ministry of External Affairs), no Commonwealth capital has anything like the turnover of Commonwealth business that London has. Moreover, the volume of work continues to grow even though the Colonial Office remains separate. The Commonwealth Relations Office deals with a large part of the world in which British interests and responsibilities are highly concentrated. In 1963–4, for example, this area accounted for about two-thirds of current British private investment overseas and some eighty-five per cent of British Government aid including technical assistance. The Plowden Report itself recognized that 'we should continue to cultivate relations with Commonwealth countries on as deep a level as possible and to take the fullest advantage of the key provided to us by the widespread use of the English language', and that 'there is a greater ease of understanding and a greater intimacy in our relationships with many Commonwealth countries than with many foreign countries'. Further, the Commonwealth service has an 'additional and special responsibility for consulting and exchanging views and information with other Commonwealth countries and for encouraging activities, both governmental and non-governmental which strengthen the Commonwealth link'. This would appear to call for a special expertise. The Labour Government, with its emphasis on Commonwealth Relations, will certainly not consider the amalgamation of the two Ministries.

Indeed, it has already promoted the Department of Technical Cooperation to the status of Ministry of Overseas Development. This has responsibility for coordinating Government policy on international aid (not just within the Commonwealth) both in terms of technical assistance and financial aid. It will undertake a scientific study of the requirements of the under-developed countries in which the specific British contribution could best be used to promote development. 'The purpose of the new Ministry . . . will be to help promote the progress of the developing countries, bearing in mind our special ties with Commonwealth countries, including the dependent territories.' The Ministry will also be responsible for the Commonwealth Development Corporation.[1]

From time to time certain Commonwealth Governments have put forward ideas for formalizing the arrangements for consultation between members, but these ideas have hitherto found little favour. The only organizations, so far, which represent all the member countries of the Commonwealth and which advise the Governments on matters of common concern, are those dealing with technical and economic questions. There has been the same reluctance to consider a permanent secretariat, with the result that there is no central clearing house. So far, since Britain's interests are universal and Britain has, for historical reasons, closer links with the Commonwealth countries than they have with one another, the greater part of the responsibility for initiating and carrying out Commonwealth consultation has rested with the Commonwealth Relations Office. However, we have already mentioned the decision of the 1964 Conference to consider a Commonwealth Secretariat and progress in this matter to date is discussed

[1] Statement by the Minister, Mrs Barbara Castle, November 10, 1964.

further below. It only remains to state that one expert on Commonwealth matters has expressed doubt whether, even if a Secretariat is established, the work of the Commonwealth Relations Office would be materially reduced 'since the need for consultation with our representatives in Commonwealth countries on matters connected with the new Secretariat's activities would remain'.[1]

We turn now to certain specific matters on which various means of consultation and cooperation have developed. Though each Commonwealth nation is responsible for its own Defence organization and there is no central coordinating agency for Commonwealth defence, there is close liaison between Governments and practical cooperation between the Services. Defence problems are, of course, frequently discussed at Prime Minister's Conferences. There are frequent exchanges of visits between British and Commonwealth Ministers concerned with defence and between senior Service officers. Service officers are generally attached as advisers on the staffs of the High Commissioners. Army chiefs of other countries attend an annual conference under the Chief of the Imperial General Staff (a *British* Government appointee) and Navy and Air Chiefs are invited to similar meetings. There is also a Commonwealth advisory Committee on Defence Science. Other examples of practical cooperation are combined exercises, joint research organizations, exchange of staff officers, technical specialists and training facilities. The Woomera Rocket Range is a joint project whose cost is shared between Britain and Australia. Equipment and training methods may be standardized. Officers and civil servants from other countries attend courses at the Imperial Defence College in London, the Joint Services Staff College in Buckinghamshire, the Royal Air Force Colleges in Britain. Some interchange takes place between countries other than Britain. Canadian and Australian students attend staff colleges in India and Pakistan; Indian and Pakistani students attend Australian and Canadian service schools; British and Canadian teams have assisted in training, e.g. the Ghanaian armed forces.

There is a full-scale military treaty between Malaysia and Britain, endorsed by Australia and New Zealand. Special arrangements were made to assist India with arms and military equip-

[1]Professor K. E. Robinson, in *Public Administration*, Vol. 42, 1964.

ment in 1962 on the occasion of the Chinese attack. There are, of course, inter-connections resulting from common membership of other organizations, e.g. Britain and Canada in NATO, Britain and Pakistan in CENTO, Britain, Australia and New Zealand in SEATO. All this, however, does not add up to general agreement on military matters throughout the Commonwealth—indeed 'non-alignment' would be incompatible with involvement in defence measures associated with the Cold War. It does mean, nevertheless, that there is little, if any, objection to the various partial arrangements from Commonwealth members not involved in them.

In economic affairs, although the Commonwealth is vitally interested in general world development, the increase of trade between Commonwealth countries is still regarded as of vital importance. Moreover, special Commonwealth relations, including the Preference System, continue to make a major if relatively diminishing contribution to development in general. All the Commonwealth countries, except Canada, belong to the Sterling Area (which, however also includes some nine non-Commonwealth countries). They keep their foreign currency reserves largely in sterling and maintain a fixed value for their currency against sterling. The transactions of the sterling area with the rest of the world are cleared in London. Other countries outside the Area, of course, also use sterling. These currency arrangements derive essentially from the close trade and financial links existing between Britain and Commonwealth countries and they continue, without any legal or formal aggreements, because they suit the convenience of the trades and countries concerned.

General Commonwealth economic problems and policies have been discussed at a series of economic conferences since the war. We quote from the Commonwealth Trade and Economic Conference held in Montreal in 1958 :

'The Commonwealth has a population of 660 million people and covers an area of 12 million square miles. The ties that hold members together reach into every part of the world and unite countries of almost every race and at almost every stage of economic development. At the one extreme there are fully industrialized and prosperous societies, while at the

48

other, large populations exist at very low levels of income. Others are at different stages between these limits. . . . But the Commonwealth countries are interdependent in that the progress of each is affected in greater or less degree by the prosperity of the others. In particular, the rapid advancement of the less-developed countries is a matter of major concern to their more prosperous partners.'

The theme of the Conference was 'an expanding Commonwealth in an expanding world'. The first result was the establishment of a Commonwealth Economic Consultative Council, consisting, at the highest level, of the Finance and Economic Ministers of the Commonwealth countries. The council meets regularly at official level and at ministerial level usually once a year. It now incorporates the Commonwealth Liaison Committee, the Commonwealth Economic Committee and meetings of Commonwealth statisticians.

Since 1932 Commonwealth countries have exchanged tariff preferences, and while there has been reduction in some duties since the war, while rising prices have reduced the effect of others, the system is maintained. However, subject to certain reservations which Britain made, international agreements forbid the creation of *new* preferences. This system, as well as other mutual arrangements, might well have been affected by Britain's entry into the European Economic Community. The 1962 Conference accordingly devoted most of its attention to the question of safeguards for Commonwealth interests. There were many differences of view and uncertainties, and although it was recognized that the final decision would be Britain's there was clearly much misgiving about the possible effect of her entry both upon the interests of particular Commonwealth members and upon the Commonwealth as a whole. The breakdown of the negotiations prevented further developments and, at least in the opinion of the Labour Party, strengthened the case for still further efforts to enlarge Commonwealth trade and economic cooperation. We refer to this again below.

Britain continues to be the main source of financial and technical assistance to other Commonwelath countries. Her annual expenditure on the provision of capital and technical assistance doubled between 1957 and 1962, reaching over £150 million in the latter year. About £130 million went in bilateral arrangements and ninety per cent of it to Commonwealth countries. There is also a substantial flow of private investment—about £150 million per annum—from Britain to developing countries in the Commonwealth, in addition to between £50 and £100 million to Canada, Australia and New Zealand. The last three countries have themselves provided assistance to developing countries on an increasing scale. There has been much mutual technical assistance in which the developing countries themselves have shared. We refer above to the 1964 proposals for considerable additions to such schemes and below to subsequent proposals by the Labour Government in 1964–5.

Two regional plans deserve mention here. The Colombo Plan covers South and South-East Asia and extends far beyond the Commonwealth countries in that area, while it also includes countries outside it altogether—Australia, Britain, Canada, New Zealand, as well as Japan and the United States. Member countries are represented on a consultative committee which meets annually to review progress and assess the tasks and problems of the area. It last met in London in 1964. Member countries in the region itself finance most of their own current development and, indeed, help each other with technical assistance. Much investment capital comes from outside the region. There is also a Technical Cooperation Plan. The whole arrangement is illustrative both of the way in which Commonwealth countries can cooperate to deal with common problems and take a leading part in their solution over a much wider area than that of the Commonwealth itself.

In 1960 a meeting of the Commonwealth Economic Consultative Council sought, through the Special Commonwealth African Assistance Plan, to focus attention on the effort of Commonwealth countries in providing aid bilaterally as well as through international organizations, and on the need for further help in meeting the urgent needs for assistance in raising living standards in the less-developed African Commonwealth countries. Britain has separate technical assistance arrangements with, for example, Ghana, Nigeria, Sierra Leone, Tanganyika, Uganda, Kenya, Malawi and Zambia.

The Commonwealth as a Whole

Although we discuss later the role of Britain in the Commonwealth, this seems a convenient place to summarize the channels through which finance from Britain flows to the overseas Commonwealth, both private and public. By private direct investment some £150 million goes annually, especially to Australia, India and the countries which made up the Federation of Rhodesia and Nyasaland. On the London market between 1946 and 1961 public authorities in the overseas Commonwealth borrowed over £300 million. Private borrowing by firms in those countries has since 1952 run at the rate of at least £40 million per annum. Commonwealth Assistance Loans, to speed up economic development, under the Export Credits Guarantee Department, have numbered over thirty to eleven different countries, seven of which were Commonwealth members; the total amounted to over £250 million. Under the Colonial Development and Welfare Acts, Britain is providing about £340 million, mostly in grants. Exchequer loans amounted to over £70 million by 1963. Dependent territories may also receive direct budgetary assistance from Britain and in 1963–4 this amounted to more than £15 million for over twenty countries. Assistance was given for such disasters as floods, earthquakes, hurricanes, and famines. The Commonwealth Development Corporation whose borrowing powers were recently increased and which is empowered to assist independent as well as dependent Commonwealth countries, has already advanced nearly £100 million and with the guidance of the new Ministry of Overseas Development will doubtless enlarge its activities. The Commonwealth Development Finance Company, whose capital is subscribed by a large number of United Kingdom firms, the Bank of England, and some Commonwealth Central Banks, has committed well over £20 million to thirty-six projects in thirteen Commonwealth countries. It must be added that Britain is a major contributor to the United Nations and its specialized agencies and some £80 million has been channelled through the International Bank for Reconstruction and development as loans in sterling Commonwealth countries. Under the Colonial Loans Acts Britain has underwritten International Bank loans to her dependencies to the value of nearly £90 million (nearly £15 million in 1961 alone). The International Bank also raises loans on the London Money Market and £46 million had been thus loaned by it to Commonwealth countries up to 1962. Britain has also agreed to contribute nearly £21 million over a period of years to the Indus Basin Development Fund.

Finally, in this connection, mention must again be made of the Department of Technical Assistance, now the Ministry of Overseas Development. Technical assistance is provided especially in the fields of economic development, administration and the social services, both to independent and dependent countries. It would be tedious to list the variety of experts who have been enabled to work in Commonwealth countries for shorter or longer periods or the various research projects financed. We have already noted the determination of the 1964 Conference to extend still further help of this nature, and the continued interest of the new Labour Government of 1964, which has given extended responsibilities to the new Ministry.

The Commonwealth is linked physically by airways, shipping routes, cable and wireless. It is interesting to note that a traveller from a Commonwealth country can travel the world entirely by Commonwealth lines which cooperate with one another. There is a Commonwealth Shipping Committee, a Commonwealth Air Transport Council, and a Commonwealth Telecommunications Board. Plans are well advanced for a Commonwealth 'round the world' coaxial telephone cable to link all the Commonwealth countries.

In an increasingly scientific world it is not surprising that the Commonwealth has paid considerable attention to science and research. The pattern of scientific cooperation was described by His Royal Highness, the Duke of Edinburgh, in an address to the Pakistan Association for the Advancement of Science in 1959, as 'the regular discussion of general scientific problems and of problems particular to the Commonwealth, and of the administration of science and research; the regular exchange of scientific cooperation; the movement of scientists; and technical help and advice'. These purposes are served by regular conferences and contacts between official research organizations; by the British Commonwealth Scientific Offices which act as points of contact between the scientific organizations of member countries for the communication of scientific ideas and information; by the Commonwealth Agricultural Bureaux which again serve as clearing houses of information and intelligence centres for scientists and research workers in agriculture and forestry; by bursaries, scholarships, lectureships and various other schemes of assisted exchange; and finally, by technical assistance schemes like the Colombo Plan. In addition to many formal conferences, like that of nuclear scientists in 1958, there are periodical meetings of the British Commonwealth Scientific Committee which consists of the heads of the national research organizations of Commonwealth countries. There have been Commonwealth Standards Conferences to discuss, for example, certification marking, engineering standards and other similar matters. Commonwealth statisticians meet frequently. There has been considerable collaboration in the field of atomic energy, particularly for development purposes, e.g. in India. The 1964 Conference showed considerable interest in the possibility of a Commonwealth space research programme. The British Overseas Research Council formulates policy in respect of scientific research overseas matters concerning scientific development in the Commonwealth which are referred to it. The Commonwealth Institute of Social Research in Ottawa is a centre for fundamental research in the social sciences and the humanities to serve the Commonwealth as a whole, though its executive is Canadian. To all this must be added schemes for collaboration in scientific research and for the interchange of science graduates and lecturers between Commonwealth countries, sponsored and financed by such bodies as the British Council, the Nuffield Foundation, and the Royal Society.

Educational links are, again, of fundamental importance. Three Commonwealth Education Conferences have been held, at Oxford (1959), New Delhi (1962) and Ottawa (1964). From these have come ever increasing interest in inter-Commonwealth cooperation, which is worked out in detail by the Commonwealth Education Liaison Committee for policy, and by the Commonwealth Education Liaison Unit functioning continuously to provide information and foster projects in the field of education. Commonwealth Scholarships and Fellowships are provided. Of the 1,000 places under the Scholarship Plan, half are held in Britain. Whether students come with scholarships, government assistance or privately, they constitute a growing link between Britain and other Commonwealth countries. In 1962 there were

Britain and the Commonwealth

40,000 Commonwealth students in Britain in universities, technical colleges and other institutions and in industry. Others were in Canada, Australia and India. Large numbers of teachers from Britain serve in schools, teacher-training colleges, technical colleges and universities in Commonwealth countries and schemes are continually being added both to increase the numbers and improve the conditions. 19,000 British citizens were serving in the Commonwealth in 1963. Canadians and New Zealanders, among others, also serve in other parts of the Commonwealth. Provision is also made in various ways for teacher-training in, for example, Britain, Canada, New Zealand, India and Pakistan. Assistance is also necessary in the field of technical education and training and again, not only Britain, but India, Pakistan and Ceylon offer facilities. In 1962 a Council for Technical Education and Training for Overseas Countries was established. In Higher Education (which in Britain means, primarily university education) there is the Association of the Universities of the British Commonwealth, a voluntary body which operates the Commonwealth University Interchange Scheme; and the Inter-University Council for Higher Education Overseas, which makes available the experience of British universities to those overseas and assists in obtaining staff to serve in Commonwealth countries. Joint appointments are made by British Commonwealth universities and many of them are linked together in various ways. In a rather more specialized field, the Bridges Committee on Training in Public Administration for Overseas Countries has led to the development of many schemes involving British universities, other bodies like the Royal Institute of Public Administration and central and local Government bodies. There are proposals for a special institution in Britain for top level training in administration 'including development and research'. Coordination of various schemes is provided through the Ministry of Overseas Development and the British Council and there is a high level Advisory Committee.

Mention must be made of Commonwealth cooperation through the Commonwealth Press Union and Commonwealth Broadcasting Conferences, and also of the Commonwealth Parliamentary Association, which has eighty branches thoughout the legislatures of the Commonwealth. There is a constant interchange of views between Commonwealth 'parliamentarians' as well as Parliamentary Conferences, now held annually. The *Journal of the Parliaments of the Commonwealth* is a continuing source of information on matters of common interest, despite the many deviations from the 'Westminster model' in Commonwealth countries. If, as a leading article in *The Times* stated on January 4, 1965, 'the function of the Commonwealth is to be found only in the work it actually does' it surely performs a great deal of work!

VIII: HOW FAR IS THE COMMONWEALTH 'BRITISH'?

It has been suggested that the Commonwealth continues only because Britain devotes a great deal of effort to maintaining it and because, clearly, she has an interest in its preservation. It should already have become clear, however, that other members also have an interest in its continuance. Indeed, they have come increasingly to display a desire to have influence proportionate to that 'equality of status' which is the starting point of Commonwealth relations. This section examines the present role of Britain in the Commonwealth and seeks to discover any evidence that this role is beginning to change.

The Commonwealth has ceased to be British in name, on a great number of issues it has ceased to respond to Britain's leadership when offered, and many of its members have demolished the structure imported from Westminster, as we show in detail in a later section. Yet one of the most perceptive of experts, Professor S.A. de Smith, could still suggest in 1964 that 'in many ways it has remained a Britannic association'.

To lawyers and parliamentarians in almost every Commonwealth country Britain is still the model. Meetings of Commonwealth Prime Ministers and Presidents have always, so far, been held in London under British chairmanship. Britain alone has a separate Commonwealth Relations Office and up till now arguments that it might be merged with the Foreign Office have been rejected. The Queen resides in London and her regular contacts are with British Ministers, although frequent tours both to her realms and to the Republics help to show from time to time that she 'belongs' to the Commonwealth. For Commonwealth countries other than Canada trading links and overseas communications are predominantly with Britain. The fact that some members think of the maintenance of the Commonwealth as being primarily a British interest is revealed by their tendency to judge Britain's conduct by especially exacting standards. Perhaps a British tendency, conversely, to regard Britain as the model and centre is shown by the tendency, in some unofficial quarters at least, to judge the conduct of new Commonwealth Governments, especially in Africa, by excessively rigid British standards. This, despite the just contention in *The Times* that 'the Commonwealth could be a unique body for understanding how . . . differences arise from different mentalities, environments, cultural approaches'.

Members have occasionally dropped hints about leaving the Commonwealth (or, in the case of Tanganyika in 1961, on the South African issue, about not seeking membership) unless a particular British policy is modified. The reaction to the Commonwealth Immigrants Act, 1962, and to Britain's application to join the Common Market, emphasized how much relations with *Britain* are identified with Commonwealth relations. 'It is therefore difficult,' says Professor de Smith, 'to subscribe to the widely-held view that in the last few years the Commonwealth has become less Anglocentric.'

Yet others have deplored changes in what they consider to be the distinctive characteristics of the 'British' Commonwealth. As perhaps an extreme, though certainly not the only example of this, we may quote Sir Roy Welensky's condemnation of what he regards as the excessive influence of African states in the Commonwealth. He has regretted the inclusion of nations with different cultures and ideologies and 'no built-in-loyalty to the Sovereign', and to whom, in his view, Commonwealth ideals are meaningless. He has even condemned the admission of Republics and would lay down rules and basic principles for membership. All this obviously implies that the Commonwealth is less 'British' than it used to be, or ought to be. Though the logic of Sir Roy's argument becomes somewhat blurred when he suggests as an 'acceptable' list of members : Australia, Canada, the United Kingdom, Malaysia, New Zealand, Nigeria, Pakistan and Rhodesia! What do these possess in common which no other existing member shares—except perhaps what appears to be Sir Roy's basic demand that members should not be neutralist'?

There are, however, two approaches revealed in the above paragraphs. The one speaks in detail about practical considerations which, so far, appear to have made almost inevitable Britain's predominant role in the new Commonwealth as in the old. The other emphasizes the changing character of the Commonwealth in more general terms and particularly from the point of view of its multi-racial character and its heterogeneity of outlook. So far as the latter is concerned, if 'one function of the Commonwealth is to be the most effective multi-racial forum', *The Times* rightly stipulates that 'for such a purpose to be breathed into the Commonwealth it must be more than a British-based, British-inspired institution'. So far as the former approach is concerned, it is necessary to examine the situation in rather more detail in order to assess the likelihood of change.

From the point of view of her historical role, and indeed, from her present position, political and economic, however changed it may be, Britain is still clearly in many ways the 'centre' of the Commonwealth. We need not repeat the importance of the English language, English traditions and approaches to the problems of government, and the links of all kinds which still to a great extent radiate from London. In so far as legislation provides advantages for citizens of the Commonwealth, as, for example, statutes which provide trustee security status for stock, or mutual recognition of professional qualifications, or reciprocal arrangements for social insurance and similar benefits, it is mainly British legislation which offers such advantages to other members. If practical assistance in a crisis is needed, Britain takes the lead, as in the case of India during the Chinese invasion (though here she was joined by Australia and Canada); still more obviously in the case of the East African countries during the army mutinies. Britain has a continuing obligation to Malaysia during the Indonesian threat. At the Commonwealth Education Conference in Ottawa in 1964 it was Britain who set the example by offering to increase her aid to £5 million per annum for five years for capital assistance. The Labour Government which assumed office in October, 1964, immediately brought into being the new Ministry of Overseas Development, not merely to expand the work of the pre-existing Department of Technical Cooperation, but also to being together the various sources of aid and to dramatize the intention to put the Commonwealth in the forefront of constructive development.

A large proportion of the practical links which were described at length in the previous section are bi-lateral rather than multilateral, although the latter type of scheme was to the forefront in discussions at the 1964 Conference. Each member still has more to do with Britain than with any other part of the Commonwealth. Ghana, for example, probably finds more in common with Nigeria on 'Commonwealth' matters than on matters discussed by the Organization of African States. The existence of a separate Commonwealth ministry in London, as the Plowden Committee pointed out, 'reflects Britain's special position as the centre of the Commonwealth'. It was for this reason that the Committee did not recommend the immediate merging of the Commonwealth Relations Office with the Foreign Office. They had in mind, interestingly enough, 'public opinion more particularly in this country than in (other) Commonwealth countries'. The Commonwealth has come into being because of other members' past connections with Britain, and survives largely because of the continued strength of these connections. Not that the relationship is at any point that of master and servant. Even if the desire on the part of Britain were there, she is far too aware of other forces at work in the world to attempt domination. The British Government wishes to preserve the Commonwealth because to do so is to underline the importance of the British connection with each other member, and also to stress the free association which they have with countries in Asia and Africa. But this does not mean that Britain can alter their views if they are determined not to be persuaded. This, of course, was equally true of the 'old Commonwealth' though there were fewer matters upon which differences of opinion were likely to arise. Nevertheless, Britain's position is still such that she remains the most powerful influence in the Commonwealth so long as she remains able to carry other members with her, either as a result of persuasion or of the concrete assistance which she can render to them.

In one way this continued predominance of Britain may appear to derive from her original role in the Empire which became the

Commonwealth. The only common foundation of the Commonwealth, it may be said, is its descent from the British Empire. Up to the Second World War its members possessed similar political systems, some degree of unity, a common military strategy and an identity of outlook on international affairs—all cemented by British direction and the broad consent of mainly British descended settlers. A great deal of this was bound to change and as the changes came the argument was advanced that the Empire was not lost but transformed. Transformed indeed it was, but in such a way that the old 'Empire Men' now regard it, to quote 'a Conservative', writing in *The Times*, as a 'gigantic farce'. Certainly, whereas the Empire was a powerful, coherent, political organization, the Commonwealth is a loose, voluntary grouping of sovereign states. Yet in many ways, as we have seen, the one undeniable link remains—Britain. 'The trouble is,' said President Nyerere of Tanzania at the 1964 Conference, 'that we are all so British. . . . Our discussions here have been so awfully "Commonwealth".' The slide from 'British' to 'Commonwealth' is significant. It must be added. however, as an indication at least of slight change, that other representatives such as Dr Banda of Malawi and Mr Margai of Sierra Leone made somewhat forceful —and perhaps less 'English!'—contributions to the discussion.

On the other hand, it has also been suggested that a distinctive feature of the Commonwealth association has been not so much its origin as an outgrowth of Empire as in the attempt to give it formal expression as a Commonwealth. With all the weaknesses and doubts which have already been expressed, so far it appears that the Commonwealth has more capacity for survival and development than the short-lived French Community.

Not that Britain, or at least a large section of the British people, has been aware of these developments, still less of their significance. It has been said that much of the public attitude in Britain has revealed an ignorance of current changes and their meaning and an emotionalism that has now ceased to accord with the facts. The Commonwealth, it is suggested, provided a 'shock absorber' for British public opinion. A generation which had grown to maturity with 'Land of Hope and Glory', a map painted red and showing one quarter of the globe as 'their Empire (on which, to recall the cliché, the 'sun never set'), would certainly have reacted more violently—like, perhaps, the French over Indo-China and North Africa—to a relative loss of power by Britain and to her changed position in the world, had it not been possible to cling to the comforting concept of 'the Commonwealth'. So, the gradual transition, under Labour and Conservative Governments alike, served a 'useful psychological purpose'. It must be added, however, that these reactions could be dangerous if they fostered illusions and produced exaggerated ideas of what Britain could or should do.

The fact is, of course, that the idea of the Commonwealth has not been the fruit only of British endeavour. It has been the creation of men living outside the United Kingdom, ranging from Canada to India and back to Nigeria and other countries. True, these 'men of independent mind' have imbibed the ideas of Burns and Cromwell, Hampden and Locke—not to mention more recent anti-imperialists like Leonard Barnes and Harold Laski. But they have used these ideas to produce in their own countries the same sense of independence and national identity as those from which they were derived. Moreover, the development of independence within the Empire-Commonwealth by the 'older Dominions', some of whom, for example Canada, were as 'nationalistic' as newer members, made the idea of Dominion Status, later independence within the Commonwealth, more palatable, indeed attractive. We have referred above to Professor Rajan's account of the further contribution made by India. It is only to be expected, therefore, that if the Commonwealth is to remain a force for the future, there will have to be greater equality in practice as well as in status and that the adjective 'British' will, to a greater or less extent, have to disappear in action as well as in speech. Mr Nehru's reference to 'our' association will have to become more meaningful.

Not all the demands for a greater say in matters when British politics might affect the interests of other Commonwealth members have come from 'recent recruits'. Indeed, to go no further back, in 1922 Canada and others, on the occasion of the notorious 'Chanak' telegram, bluntly repudiated the policy of Prime Minister Lloyd George which seemed likely to provoke war with Turkey. It is said that in 1956 the strongest telegram ever sent within the Commonwealth was that from Mr St Laurent, Canadian Prime Minister, to Mr Eden, British Prime Minister, on the Suez issue. Nevertheless more recent developments have emphasized the probability that newer members—whose 'hatred . . . for imperialism is far more vociferous and disruptive than anything felt by Canada or Australia', to quote *The Times*—might seek a more continuing influence over British (and general Commonwealth) policies. Tanganyika's announcement that she would not seek admission to the Commonwealth if South Africa remained a member was only the sharpest reminder till then that whatever Britain's desire she could not assume that other members would go along with her. Again, in 1963, when hopes were high that an East African Federation might come into being, Tanganyika and Uganda urged the British Government to speed up independence for Kenya. We have already emphasized the deep concern of many African, as well as other members, over the situation in Southern Rhodesia. There is good reason to believe that the British attitude was greatly influenced by the evidence that most Members were determined not to recognize a unilateral declaration of independence by the Southern Rhodesian Government and that a real attempt should be made to arrange a conference, including African leaders, with a view to constitutional reform. There is also good reason to believe that unless these viewpoints had to a large extent been met, the Commonwealth might have broken up under the strain or at least lost many of its members. Indeed, the 1964 Conference has been described as facing the fourth 'great crisis' in the history of the Empire-Commonwealth— the other three being, according to this interpretation, the American War of Independence, the new position created during the birth-pangs of the Dominion of Canada in 1867 (when federation appeared the only possible solution to gradual absorption by the United States), and the decision of India to become a republic in 1949. The statement of one constitutional expert (made before 1964) that 'Britain might be obliged as a matter of practical politics to take into account the known attitudes of other members' certainly turned out to be correct.

Indeed, Prime Minister Wilson carried the implications of all this somewhat further. Having decided to send a strong letter to Mr Ian Smith, Premier of Southern Rhodesia, after the latter's refusal to allow the Commonwealth Secretary to see African leaders in detention if he visited the Colony, he went beyond the normal protocol of 'informing' other Commonwealth capitals through normal diplomatic channels. To his appeal for support in his attitude, Mr Pearson (Canada), Mr Holyoake (New Zealand), Mr Shastri (India), Tunku Abdul Rahman (Malaysia) and others sent unequivocal support—of which, doubtless, Mr Smith was aware. For whatever reason, he began, at least temporarily, to play down the issue of immediate independence. It will be noticed that 'old' and 'new' members participated in this 'warning'.

The Queen's Speech in 1964, expressing the Government's policy, had, in fact, referred to 'the unique role of the Commonwealth'. Yet it still appears that Britain's role remains, if not unique, decisive. The long-term significance of the events described, however, must not be overlooked. Indeed, for some time now there has been strong feeling even in Britain that the Commonwealth must become less United Kingdom-centred. In March, 1964 the Plowden Report recorded the opinion that it was high time Britain and the Commonwealth shed 'the mother country' fixation and made the relationships of members one of real as well as constitutional equality. True, the Report did suggest that any move immediately to merge the Commonwealth Relations and Foreign Offices might be 'misunderstood' as a loss of interest in the Commonwealth, though it adduced little evidence to support its contention. But the previously quoted general sentiment expressed what others had long felt.

Indeed, one of the greatest surprises of the 1964 Conference was the pressure from the newer members, particularly President Nkrumah (Ghana), President Kenyatta (Kenya) and Prime Minister Williams (Trinidad and Tobago)—strong enough to convert Prime Minister Pearson (Canada) from reluctance to enthusiastic support—for a Commonwealth Secretariat. This is so important as to merit full consideration, although at the time of writing (January, 1965) it had not yet come into being.

The newer members clearly felt the need for such a central organ, partly as a body which would complete the process of 'decolonization' by taking the management of the Commonwealth out of the hands of Britain. In so far as the Commonwealth has been 'run' at all, it has been through the Commonwealth Relations Office which has arranged conferences, kept up a stream of information and performed whatever administrative tasks arose out of decisions taken. Despite the fact that this appeared to indicate to many 'that Britain remained the hub of the wheel and . . . that only British effort and ingenuity kept the Commonwealth breathing at all', it had been assumed that the arrangement met with Commonwealth wishes. Such a view was laid to rest in 1964. Clearly there was discontent with British administration. Although London, as the biggest capital, with unrivalled facilities, and best situated for the growing dealings with Europe as well as for contacts with America, was still seen as the natural centre for organizing Commonwealth affairs, the Commonwealth Relations Office was no longer seen as the right Secretariat.

The Commonwealth, it was felt, needed a body which the Commonwealth as a whole would staff, control, and own. The terms of reference given to the conference of senior officials under the chairmanship of Sir Burke Trend, Secretary to the British Cabinet, may, at first sight, appear narrow. They are asked to make proposals for a secretariat which would disseminate factual information to all member countries on matters of common concern, assist existing agencies, both official and unofficial, in the promotion of Commonwealth links in all fields; and help to coordinate, in cooperation with the host country, the preparation for future meetings of Commonwealth Heads of Governments and, where appropriate, for meetings of other Commonwealth Ministers'. But, as *The Times* remarked, this 'could justify a substantial agency carrying out extensive functions, many of which are now scattered between British government departments, Commonwealth High Commissions, and many voluntary bodies. . . . There is everything to be said for giving the secretariat, as a multi-national body, the widest executive powers possible'.[1]

The same officials are also to consider the proposal for a Commonwealth Foundation. This idea, first suggested in Mr Gordon Walker's book on the Commonwealth, endorsed in principle at the 1964 Conference, and now part of the programme to 'revitalize' the Commonwealth, would create an interchange network to ensure closer liaison between, for example, the British Medical

[1] I am indebted for much of the above to *The Times* leading article, 4 January, 1965.

Association and similar medical associations in the other Commonwealth countries, and, indeed between a large number of professional and technological organizations.

To return to our general theme, foreign observers who are knowledgeable about British politics may find some cause for wonder at the lead taken by a Labour Government in Commonwealth matters, though they would perhaps recall that a considerable majority of the Conservative Party was prepared to take Britain into the Common Market in 1962 despite many Commonwealth misgivings, while the Labour Party insisted that firm conditions should be laid down to safeguard Commonwealth interests and, indeed, that the Commonwealth might provide an alternative means of economic and trade progress. This latter point has again been emphasized in Prime Minister Wilson's early activities. A 'trade-and-aid' plan was immediately put under discussion through the Board of Trade and the Ministry of Overseas Development.

Although it would be inaccurate to suggest that the Conservative Party has ceased to be Commonwealth-minded, or that the Labour Party can seriously believe that all Britain's—certainly not all world-problems—can be solved through the Commonwealth, since divisions of opinion about the present Commonwealth and its future cut across party lines, it is interesting to note changing opinions on this subject. Some pertinent remarks are contained in Professor Rajan's book already referred to earlier.

'It is perhaps largely because of this great transformation of the Commonwealth that influential sections of public opinion in parts of the Commonwealth, especially in Great Britain, have switched over from their former proprietary and paternal attitude to the Commonwealth to one of treating the Commonwealth as an outgrown child for whom they have little responsibility or in whom they have little interest. Since the present Commonwealth ceased to be a British family of nations, and which Great Britain, their mother country, no longer dominates, but has become a multi-racial, multi-cultural and multi-lingual Commonwealth, they seem to have chosen to disown it, even if a little reluctantly. They are apparently not content to acknowledge a mere share in the creation of the present Commonwealth and be proud of it. Because the present Commonwealth is not *entirely* the creation of Great Britain and the old Dominions, they do not care to own it as their own. In consequence, they do not seem to want the preservation and promotion of the Commonwealth and its interests to be as decisively important as it used to be until now in their country's role in world affairs.'

That there is a great deal in these charges cannot be denied. But it is not an easy task to assess the likely strands of opinion in the face of, in the long run, a relative diminution in the unilateral significance of Britain. We merely attempt some simple assessments. Among informed people the process will doubtless be regarded with positive pleasure. When a journal such as the *Economist* can argue that we should get rid of the notion of a 'family' or at least of 'maternalism', and even that the word 'loyal' should be expunged from the vocabulary of Commonwealth discourse, the 'Empire-men' need not be feared. But what of the 'general public'?

First it must be said that normally its members show little knowledge of or interest in Commonwealth affairs. There are few 'votes' to be gained from either fostering Commonwealth relations or to be lost by making mistakes or even causing disasters in colonial policy. Nor does the average man or woman appear to attach much importance to the 'Commonwealth'. Ignorance about it is surprisingly wide-spread. 'Knowledge' is often based on rumour, half-truths, or prejudice. There can be an upsurge of feeling about 'Mau Mau' outrages in Kenya, though attention is focused on the few whites affected by atrocities and much less on the far more numerous African victims. It is perhaps significant that the really 'newsworthy' items from the Congo are again those affecting the fate of white people. A Suez expedition will produce, especially among the less-educated, a desire to teach 'the wogs' a lesson. If there be any truth in the charge that the British have been consoling themselves for their reduced status by setting up a 'fantasy Empire' in which Britain's supposed 'moral example does duty for the gunboat of yesteryear', it is equally true that there is great relief when, momentarily, a gunboat is used again.

As for the moral example, a large proportion of British people seem unaware that this cannot be asserted successfully if colour-prejudice is allowed to appear and even—so it has been argued—to affect the results of certain elections. The Americans, however much some of them fail to live up to the precept, now at least realize that without a solution of their Negro problem they can scarcely expect to win sympathy and support in the non-white countries of the world. The British—or at least responsible rulers —may realize that they cannot support white-minority regimes abroad, though many of them would undoubtedly respond to the call of 'Kith and Kin' from white residents in Southern Rhodesia. They have yet to realize that landladies who deny rooms to coloured students may be offending the future rulers of Commonwealth countries. And that the Commonwealth Immigrants Act of 1962, whatever its intention and, perhaps, even justification in the absence of more satisfactory ways of controlling immigration (which, indeed, every other Commonwealth country does), has, in fact, operated so as to discriminate against Commonwealth citizens (while leaving the Southern Irish, who are not even members of the Commonwealth unrestricted!). But, then, a large majority of such British are probably unaware of the fact that, for example, Nigerians and Pakistani *are* Commonwealth citizens and that the normal language of, for example, West indians, is English.

These difficulties at home in Britain are certainly not unconnected with the problem of the Commonwealth as a whole. But to tell those who display such attitudes that they might well weaken the Commonwealth is of little avail, since they are also probably unaware of just how important to Britain the maintenance of the Commonwealth is. Certainly, the Commonwealth must be multi-racial, not merely in its membership but in its joint activities and responsibilities, or nothing. In this sense the role of Britain is changing and must continue to change.

Constitutions and Governments

I : THE 'WESTMINSTER MODEL' AND ITS VARIANTS

In this section our purpose is first to describe the basic features of those systems of government within the Commonwealth which are, broadly, like the 'Westminster model'; secondly, to discuss some of the more interesting 'deviations' from the model, whether constitutional, like the Presidential variations, or political, like the variations in party systems; thirdly, to attempt to assess prospects for the future of 'parliamentary democracy' in the Commonwealth.

Although this book is primarily concerned with the independent members of the Commonwealth, it may be of interest to those not familiar with the process to outline briefly the way in which independence is achieved by a dependency. Moreover, constitutional development has taken the form of a gradual transition from Crown Colony government to a system of responsible Cabinet government and almost every member has started life as an independent state with a Westminster-type system of government whose emergence appears to have something of the inevitability of an evolutionary process. The reason for this has not been the insistence of Britain as the Colonial Power but rather the refusal of colonial nationalists to be put off with what they regarded as inferior brands of government. On the other hand, in many cases, soon after independence there have been 'mutations' which are not only interesting in themselves but raise the question of the future of the Commonwealth at least so far as the possession of 'common political ideals' and a 'common political idiom' are concerned.

The final stage in the progress towards full self-government is the removal of all discretionary powers exercised by the Governor and the assimilation of his position virtually to that of the Queen in the United Kingdom in the sense that he must thenceforward act on the advice of his ministers. Accordingly, we shall look first at his position before independence and take as an example the last pre-independence constitution of Nyasaland (Malawi) in 1961. That of Northern Rhodesia (Zambia) in 1962 was very similar. We may then see just what restrictions had to be removed in order that as independent states Malawi might qualify for a seat at the Commonwealth Conference of 1964 and Zambia be acknowledged as the next new member. In passing, it may be noticed that the fact that Malawi remained a constitutional monarchy with Dr Hastings Banda as Prime Minister, while Zambia started life immediately as a Republic under President Kaunda, is, in this context, irrelevant.

The Governor, until independence, was at once the Queen's representative, appointed on the advice of a Secretary of State, and the head of the government. He was obliged to consult the Executive Council (dominated by Dr Banda's Malawi Congress Party) on the formulation of policy and in the exercise of all his legal powers save those, broadly, where he might act in his discretion or under royal instructions. But he could disregard the Council's advice, though he must then report the full circumstances to the Secretary of State. He could appoint and remove members of the Council, though he had to take into account 'the composition of the parties in the Legislative Council' and consult with party leaders. He assigned responsibilities to members and controlled the agenda.

He had ceased to be a member of the Legislative Council, but he could address it at any time (and express his own views, not, as in Britain, merely read a 'Queen's Speech' which, in fact, is an exposition of Government policy). The Speaker was appointed by the Governor who also approved the Council's standing orders. He fixed the dates of sessions, prorogued and dissolved the Council. He exercised the initiative in legislation through his ministers. Certain Bills, including those concerning taxation, could not be proceeded with without his recommendation. He could refuse assent to a Bill (the royal 'veto', which has not been exercised in

Britain since Queen Anne!) or reserve it for the signification of Her Majesty's pleasure (i.e. that of the British Government). Certain Bills he was obliged to reserve. The Crown, on the advice of a Secretary of State, could disallow any Act even though it had received the Governor's assent. The Governor could, in certain circumstances, though with a report to the Secretary of State, declare any Bill introduced but not passed to have effect as if passed by the Council (the power of 'certification'). Most of these powers, of course, were used very rarely indeed, but they existed as limits even upon internal self-government.

The Governor, further, had full control over the civil service, though he could delegate his powers to an advisory Public Service Commission. He retained control of the police. He decided whether to initiate proceedings to secure the removal of a superior judge and whether to suspend him during inquiry. There were other minor powers. Finally, he could proclaim a state of emergency and acquire virtually autocratic legislative and executive powers. Presidents could learn everything they needed to know from the example of the Governor! Indeed, Mr Patrick Gordon Walker has said that President Ayub of Pakistan virtually reverted to the system of government in operation before independence in 1947.

We turn now to the process of transfer of powers during the final stages of progress towards independence. Firstly, of course, there would be the diminution of the Governor's discretionary powers. This might mean either a gradual sharing of these powers with responsible ministers or a big jump to virtual independence. In the end, slowly or quickly, there would be a significant transfer of powers from the Governor to responsible ministers, with protection for the public services from political interference. During the whole of this period the *actual* power and influence of the Governor will vary with circumstances and personalities and with the extent to which the Secretary of State urged a loosening of control or himself exercised supervision over the manner and degree of its use. It may be that as independence is approaching and a strong nationalist movement is achieving power, the Governor's personal influence will be more important than his actual powers. But he still cannot alter the constitution itself (however much it may be modified in typically British fashion by convention). This must be done by the Crown (i.e. Her Majesty's Government) and eventually by Act of the Imperial Parliament.

The Governor will have some influence (sometimes progressive, sometimes resistant) over the timing and extent of constitutional changes. But the Secretary of State and the British Government will have the last word. He will almost certainly consult local opinion and not merely accept the Governor's assessment of the situation. Such consultation may be informal or through a local committee or a commission or a parliamentary delegation or a combination of these. The final stage is likely to be a constitutional conference in London, though the Secretary of State may have to endeavour to impose a solution of his own in case of deadlock. Generally, however, 'the dynamics of colonial nationalism will normally have created a situation in which he must be an umpire, a time-keeper, a conciliator and a candid friend', as Professor S.A. de Smith has put it. In recent years his main object has been to secure aggreement on certain kinds of constitutional provisions which are thought desirable to ensure, as far as possible, parliamentary democracy and the rule of law. We shall see later how far this effort has met with more than temporary success.

We have described in general terms the change from dependence to independence. But between the two there are various degrees of 'internal self-government'. This latter, in broad terms, implies a status which falls short of full international personality (for example, it does not carry with it membership of the United Nations) and of 'Statute of Westminster' legal status. External affairs will normally be excluded from local control, though, as with the earlier 'self-governing colonies', there may be some freedom so far as trading agreements are concerned. Control over defence is usually retained by the United Kingdom by one device or another. Such control often involves considerable influence over certain aspects of social and economic life. Bills concerning external affairs or defence must always be 'reserved' by the Governor. These specific limitations are in addition to the general discretionary powers (even in internal affairs) described above. They are, of course, the modern counterpart of the Durham Report's distinction between 'local' and 'imperial' matters. Nevertheless, within the self-governing field itself the Governor's relationships with ministers will approximate to those of a Governor-General of an independent country with the Cabinet.

He will normally cease to summon, preside over, or even attend Council-Cabinet meetings. Other *ex officio* (i.e. civil service) members of the former Council of Ministers will be withdrawn. A Prime Minister or Premier will control Council-Cabinet proceedings, though he will have to keep the Governor informed. Such Prime Ministers will normally be appointed in accordance with the constitutional conventions operating in Britain (and these may be written into the Independence Constitution). He will appoint, remove, and assign departmental responsibilities to ministers. They will be individually and collectively responsible to the (lower house of the) legislature. There are, again, however, many possible transitional arrangements which we may examine briefly.

The Governor's Executive Council, originally consisting of officials and with purely advisory functions, will gradually become a Cabinet. Nominated 'unofficials' may be introduced at the Governor's discretion and representative groups may be consulted before such nomination. An elective element may next be included, chosen from the Legislative Council. Then 'unofficials' plus elected members may be given a majority, which eventually becomes a majority of elected members alone even if 'unofficials' remain. In time, the Governor and the *ex-officio* members will disappear. Sometime during this process a ministerial system will be introduced, a 'Chief Minister' (or 'Leader of Government Business') will be appointed and collective responsibility will be established. Meanwhile, the discretionary powers of the Governor will gradually be limited. The final move (unless it has already occurred during the transition) involves the advancement of the Chief Minister and Council of Ministers to the usual titles of Prime Minister and Cabinet, the complete removal of all officials (who then become Permanent Heads of Departments under political Ministers) including the last to go usually (apart from the Governor)—the Chief Secretary, the Attorney-General and the Financial Secretary.

There are similar stages, though usually occurring somewhat earlier, so far as the legislature is concerned, but the details are far too complicated to be given here. Suffice it to say that the

71

official majority usually disappears from the Legislative Council long before it goes in the Executive Council, though an *elected majority* (as opposed to one made up of 'unofficials' or of 'unofficials' plus elected members) is usually not established until at least some elected members have been appointed to the Executive Council. This is to achieve some degree of harmony between the two bodies and to avoid the executive-legislative deadlock which Lord Durham found in Canada in the 1830s. The Governor ceases to preside in the Legislative Council at a fairly early stage, but the other *ex officio* members remain in it so long as they remain in the Executive Council. As self-government approaches the nominated unofficials play a diminishing part as the elective element is enlarged, particularly if the latter belong to a powerful political party. If nominated members are required at a later stage—and this is usually only in an Upper House—they will generally be appointed by the Prime Minister.

Various special devices such as indirect elections, franchises based on particular qualities of property, education, income or status, and communal rolls or reserved seats will go once the principle of majority rule has been accepted and if the dominant political forces object to them. (Some of them, of course, like indirect elections, may be re-introduced, as we shall see in the case of Pakistan.) Most of what Disraeli called 'fancy franchises' have been used in multi-racial societies like those of East and Central Africa (they still prevail in Southern Rhodesia, together with separate 'rolls') in order to give predominant influence to Europeans. Mass political parties naturally press for universal suffrage, single-member constituencies and the 'first past the post system' unless, as we shall see later, they turn to other devices in order to ensure the continuance of their own predominance. Eventually, as these changes proceed, the Legislative Council will become a Legislature or National Assembly—or Parliament (though the original body may persist, though in changed form, as a Second Chamber). It will control its own procedures, elect its own Speaker, and be prorogued or dissolved on the advice of ministers or the Prime Minister as in the United Kingdom. The power of 'certification' will go and Bills will not be passed over the Assembly's head. The Governor's 'veto', his power to 'reserve' Bills and the Crown's power of disallowance will dwindle and virtually disappear.

There will also be changes in respect of the public services as independent government is achieved. The advisory Public Service Commission will become executive, subject usually to some ministerial control over the selection of Permanent Secretaries and other top officials. Compensation schemes will be drawn up for Overseas Civil Servants who may not wish to continue under the new system of ministerial responsibility in which there will be 'no more Civil Masters', as Dr Nkrumah once put it. Eventually, control of the police force will be transferred. There will almost certainly be a Judicial Service Commission and provision will be made for security of tenure for judges, to prevent removal on political grounds. An attempt will be made to insulate the process of public prosecution from political influence. There will also be strict procedures laid down for the authorization of public expenditure and such like matters, with protection for certain salaries, again to prevent political discrimination. Many of these safeguards, as we shall see, may be removed when full independence is achieved.

Those who believe that the Commonwealth is, or should be, based upon certain common principles and practice naturally hope that these features of the 'Westminster model' which, be it said again, are demanded by the nationalist politicians, will be preserved when full independence is achieved. Dr Nkrumah has written that 'in our struggle for freedom, parliamentary democracy was as vital an aim as independence'. Certain limitations might be removed, certain practices changed, but the basic features should, so this school of thought holds, be preserved, if the Commonwealth is to be preserved. The rest of this section examines in more detail the main features of the 'Westminster model' and its variants and the extent to which Commonwealth countries have deviated from it, as a prelude to an attempt to assess future possibilities.[1]

---

[1] For a more detailed account of the 'transfer of power' cf Professor S.A. de Smith's *op. cit.* Chapter 2, and the author's *The Cabinet in the Commonwealth.*

II : SOME FEATURES OF COMMONWEALTH
GOVERNMENTS

Some contrasting statements provide a fitting introduction to this
consideration of the separate constitutions and systems of government in the Commonwealth. In a Central Office of Information
pamphlet, *Parliamentary Government in the Commonwealth*
(1961) it is stated that

> 'fundamental to every member country is a belief in the
> concept of democratic self-government through freely elec-
> ted representatives, practised in almost all countries in the
> form known as the parliamentary system . . . Most demo-
> cratic systems, wherever practised, are derivations or
> variants of the parliamentary system as it has evolved in the
> United Kingdom . . . At all stages of British overseas expan-
> sion a close relationship existed between the pattern of
> government in Britain and that in the settlement colonies
> . . . Moreover, when the United Kingdom became respon-
> sible for the administration of overseas territories in predom-
> inantly indigenous populations, it tended to develop institu-
> tions similar to those of the United Kingdom . . . Common-
> wealth countries in Asia and Africa . . . all began their inde-
> pendence with systems of government closely patterned on
> that of the United Kingdom . . . Such is the flexibility of the
> device of responsible parliamentary government that varia-
> tions to suit local conditions can usually be made without
> affecting its fundamental characteristics. The essentials of
> the system of responsible government . . . have been largely
> preserved in the other member countries of the Common-
> wealth . . . The executive is drawn from the leadership of the
> majority party in Parliament . . . (There is) . . . close control
> of the executive over legislation and expenditure; . . . recog-
> nition of the rights of opposition parties; the anonymity
> and political independence of civil servants; and the 'rule of
> law', by which every person, including Members of Parlia-
> ment and officials, is subject to the ordinary law adminis-

tered by an independent judiciary'. (The Pamphlet has a brief appendix describing 'some modifications to the parliamentary system in Pakistan, Ghana and Cyprus'.)

Whatever criticism may be made of this statement it certainly does not fall into the self-centred view, criticized by Mr Patrick Gordon Walker, that today, in respect of Africa, 'as in the past in regard to India and the Crown Colonies . . . parliamentary democracy is suited only to Commonwealth countries with populations of European origin, and that other Commonwealth countries should evolve constitutional forms more suited to them'— and, perhaps, accept less than full self-governing status, an implication often contained in such views. This seemed, to Mr Gordon Walker, 'an arrogant attitude' that is related to the original 'British' concept of the Commonwealth. 'It implies that there is . . . an inner ring of Commonwealth countries that can alone manage to maintain effective parliamentary democracy and which will be bound together by special links of affinity that arise from it'. He goes on to recall that parliamentary democracy can collapse or be superseded, but *not for racial reasons;* it broke down in Germany in 1933 and in France in 1959. Further, whether or not parliamentary democracy is in danger in certain Commonwealth countries, it is deep-rooted in many of them which are not of European origin and is generally regarded by them as the higher form of government. Let us quote just two African politicians.

First, Dr Azikiwe in his inaugural address as Governor-General of Nigeria in 1960. 'Representative democracy . . . is based on the concepts of the rule of law and respect for individual freedom, . . (It) has been tried in Nigeria and it has worked successfully . . . (It) is not only capable of being exported to Africa, but practicable in this part of Africa'. Second, Dr Busia, exiled rival of Dr Nkrumah in Ghana. 'It is often said that Western democracy is unsuitable for Africa and alien to African thought and way of life. Others argue that in the initial phases of building up a country economically, dictatorship is more efficient . . . Both views are profoundly wrong'. Nevertheless, President Azikiwe was clearly perturbed by the course of events in Nigeria in 1964 and Dr Busia is still in exile, while his rival appears to have some sympathy at least with the view that the parliamentary system needs modifications to suit present African conditions. We must therefore enquire whether the Central office of Information picture remains completely accurate and whether the high hopes of the other authorities we have quoted are being realized.

Since 1961 the number of independent members of the Commonwealth has grown from twelve to twenty. Of these, five are Federations (though two of these existed before 1945 and were not incompatible with the features of parliamentary cabinet government); nine are Republics, all except India, Nigeria and Uganda with Presidents of the American or Fifth French Republic types or a mixture of both; one (Malaysia) has its own elective constitutional monarch, while the other ten are monarchies (realms). Some ten have an American or continental type Bill of Rights which the traditionalist constitutional lawyer, Professor A.V. Dicey for long persuaded the British was alien to their constitution. At least seven have one-party or one dominant party systems and in some opposition parties or potential oppositions have few, if any, rights. Preventive Detention Acts and similar restrictive measures abound and are no more compatible with the rule of law than when Britain herself used them in her dependent territories.

It is not surprising therefore that *The Times* leading article quoted earlier suggests that.

> 'the political unlikeness, or incompatibility, of Commonwealth members is now its most obvious feature. Neither democracy nor even acceptance of the rule of law is a common denominator . . . To outsiders it may seem unreal for the Commonwealth to exist at the level of technical aid or education, when in some states there are forms of personal rule, denial of free speech or a free press, political and even racial indoctrination, which are anathema to the others'.

Yet although 'these differences look fatal', the article went on to justify the Commonwealth. It 'could be a unique body for understanding how these differences arise from different mentalities, environments, cultural approaches. (It) exists as a repository of ideas and experiments that may continue when individual regimes change.' Finally, as we have continually emphasized, it is 'the most effective multi-racial forum and it could be made more effective in several practical ways.' But we must return to our description of the parliamentary cabinet form of government.

III : WRITTEN CONSTITUTIONS AND PARLIAMENTARY DEMOCRACY IN THE COMMONWEALTH

It is one of the fascinating ironies of politics that Britain, which has no 'written constitution' in the continental or American sense of a document setting out the fundamental principles and laws according to which the state is governed, such constitution usually being protected by the requirement of special procedures for changing it, and also by the power of the courts to interpret it, has been responsible for more written constitutions than any other country in the world. The constitutions of most Commonwealth countries began as Acts of the United Kingdom Parliament passed at the request of local legislatures after agreements as to the form and timing of independence. Many, of course, such as India, Pakistan and Ghana, have subsequently developed their own (republican) constitutions. In many cases these Acts of Parliament have actually incorporated rules governing the operation of the cabinet system which in Britain have remained a matter of convention. Moreover, as already mentioned, they have sometimes included statements of fundamental rights which 'with us', as Professor Dicey put it, were 'derived from the ordinary law of the land'.

In the parliamentary system, whether monarchial as in Britain, Canada, Australia, New Zealand, Ceylon, Sierra Leone, Jamaica, Trinidad and Tobago, Malawi, the Gambia and Malaysia (with its own monarch), or republican as in India, Nigeria and Uganda, there is a separation between the Head of State and the Head of Government. In the last three the President is, so to speak, an 'elected constitutional monarch', like the Presidents of the Third and Fourth French Republics. Such Heads of State, whether Monarchs or Presidents, have strictly limited and mainly formal functions, though their influence and powers vary both in law and practice. In the monarchial member states of the Common-

77

wealth, except Malaysia with her own constitutional monarch elected for a period by and from the Sultans of the States, the Queen is represented by a Governor-General. In the Republican-Presidential regimes of Pakistan, Ghana, Cyprus, Tanzania, Kenya and Zambia, the two roles of Head of State and Head of Government are combined as in the United States, though their constitutions also possess some of the features of the Fifth French Republic where, although President de Gaulle is Head of State and, in practice, Head of Government, there is also a Prime Minister and a Cabinet, dependent on support in the National Assembly. Parliamentary democracy requires the Head of State to be above party controversy, while power is exercised by Prime Minister and cabinet through elected representatives in Parliament. In Presidential regimes actual power is exercised by the President, though he may be checked and limited by the separate legislature. For the moment, unless the context otherwise indicates, we shall deal with the parliamentary cabinet system, whether monarchial or republican.

Legislatures may be unicameral or bicameral. In the latter case the popularly elected House, usually known as the Lower House, is legislatively and financially predominant and in parliamentary systems the Government is formed from the party or coalition of parties which has a numerical majority in the House, though some members of the Government may be taken from the Upper House. The Lower House is normally elected for a period of years by universal adult suffrage, freely exercized by secret ballot at periodical elections. It may usually be dissolved by the Head of State on the advice of the Prime Minister.

The Upper House is sometimes required as a means of protecting the units in the Federal system as in Canada, Australia, India, Malaysia and Nigeria. While the Lower House is usually elected on a population basis the Upper House may provide for equal representation of the units or at least for representatives who will protect the interests of such units. In Canada, Senators are appointed for life to the Upper House. In other countries they may be elected by a different system or in different constituencies from members of the Lower House, or, sometimes, by the Legislatures of the component units—States in Australia, India and Malaysia, Provinces in Canada, Regions in Nigeria. The Upper

House is, of course, not the only protection for such units since powers are, by the constitution, divided between the Federal or Central Government and the Government of the units. Residual powers not specified in the constitution may be left to the federal government (Canada and India) or to the units (Australia, Nigeria, Malaysia—although in the latter Malaya had a quasi-unitary constitution until joined by Singapore, British Borneo and Sarawak.)

Parliamentary cabinet government requires that ministers, who are heads of the executive departments (save for those who are 'ministers without portfolio' i.e., without specific departments but available for general duties and advice) and who are also responsible for policy and for most legislative proposals as well as finance, should be responsible to Parliament. The United Kingdom requirement that they be actual members of the legislature, however, does not always follow and ministers may sometimes speak, though not vote, in both Houses. Even when the legislature is an extremely powerful and influential body (which, as we shall see, is not always the case) it does not directly govern the country. It watches and criticises the executive government and may in the last resort defeat it and compel either resignation or dissolution and an election. The likelihood of such defeat, however, will depend largely on the nature of the party-system.

The parliamentary system on the United Kingdom model presupposes the existence of at least two parties; some would say that it can operate successfully only if there are no more than two major parties, one of which can normally achieve an overall majority in the Lower House. They would also add, however, that each of the two major parties must have a real chance of winning an election and must be regarded as an 'alternative government'. Clearly, therefore, they would argue that parliamentary democracy is incompatible with a one-party system and is not in a healthy state when one party is so dominant that no other can ever hope to replace it. We look at examples of such situations later.

When there are only two major parties each must be a coalition of different interests and opinions; indeed, in a Federal State each must include representatives of the various units if these are to feel that their interests are safeguarded. But these different interests in the party must agree on a common policy, work together in support of the party's aims, remain loyal to party decisions and maintain a united front on major issues. On the other hand, if such unity is monolithic, there is, as we suggested above, less likelihood that a government majority will be overthrown and therefore the power of the executive is greatly enhanced. Protection of minorities will then depend on the spirit in which government is carried on and, in particular, freedom of speech and meeting and free elections. Conversely, some states have adopted a virtual one-party system precisely because with a number of smaller parties, none of which by itself or in coalition can maintain power for long enough to achieve results, the needs of the country, it is felt, cannot be met.

It must be repeated, however, that it seems difficult to maintain a system of parliamentary democracy (whatever may be said of the existence of democratic discussions and procedures *within* the one party) when there is no opposition to the Government in Parliament and no possibility of a peaceful change of government. Many countries, indeed, recognize the formal rights of the Opposition, not only by safeguarding its position through the Speaker and the procedure of the Lower House, but even by paying a salary to its leader. Canada was the first to do this, Australia followed in 1920, the United Kingdom in 1937 and New Zealand in 1951. In 1964 the United Kingdom introduced payment for the Opposition leader in the House of Lords also. One-party regimes do not, of course, provide such facilities. Even where more than one party exists it has sometimes been felt unwise to encourage opposition parties where they are based on tribal or ethnic groups which, by definition, can scarcely hope to provide an 'alternative government' and whose opposition may be destructive rather than constructive. Dr Nkrumah felt this strongly in Ghana soon after independence and before a Presidential one-party regime was established.

We spoke of two major parties and this is the normal pattern in the United Kingdom, Canada (at federal, though not at provincial level), and New Zealand. In Australia the alternatives are the Labour Party (though there is a break-away group, the Democratic Party) and a coalition of the Liberal and Country

Parties which, however, do not normally oppose each other at elections. In India there is one major party, the Congress Party, which has won all federal elections but cannot always win majorities or even control majority-coalitions in all the States. Ceylon has suffered from a proliferation of parties and very uncertain government majorities; as recently as 1964 Mrs Bandaranaike's Government was defeated by the desertion of a few members of her coalition. In Malaysia there is a dominant coalition group of Malays—Chinese—Indians, which has remained in power since independence, though in Singapore, before it joined the Malayan Federation, there were several parties and changes of power. In Nigeria there have been three main parties, one in each Region (until the Acton Group in the Western Region split in 1962), and from independence to 1964 the Federal Government was based on a North-East Coalition which was increasingly restive. In 1964 the coalition finally broke up and two rival alliances faced each other, the one predominantly Northern with some allies in the South, the other predominantly Southern. At the time of writing (Jan. 1965), after disputed elections, a considerable boycott and some violence, the predominantly Northern Alliance had won a majority of seats (though many were uncontested as a matter of deliberate protest), and after some critical delay a 'broad-based' coalition emerged. Nigeria therefore provided an example of virtual one-party government in each Region and an uneasy coalition of parties at the Federal level with no obvious 'alternative government' at either level. In some other countries of the Commonwealth there has been a tendency towards one-party rule, whether by voluntary merging, as in Kenya and Uganda, or pressure, as in Malawi, or both. We deal with this phenomenon in more detail in our consideration of individual countries such as Ghana and Tanzania.

Clearly, a workable party system demands certain pre-conditions of tolerance. On the one hand, it has been said that 'it is the balance of parties which gives stability and prevents too frequent changes of government; it is the party system which reduces to a minimum the intrigues, bargainings and understandings, which in a House of petty groups or independents are apt to become an essential preliminary to every parliamentary decision'. On the other 'our parliamentary system will work so long as the

F   81

responsible people in different parties accept the view that it is better that the other side should win than that the constitution should be broken'. Provided, of course, that no party claims the tolerance enshrined in the constitution in order to achieve power merely in order to bend the constitution to its own purposes should it win.

The spirit of parliamentary government, including the maintenance of minority and opposition rights, is seen pre-eminently in the procedure of Parliament. Throughout the Commonwealth where parliamentary forms are preserved, although each legislature has adopted standing orders to suit itself, the model has been that of Britain, and everywhere 'Erskine May' (i.e., Sir T. Erskine May's *Treatise on the Law, Privileges, Proceedings and Usages of Parliament,* originally written in 1844 and kept up to date by successive Clerks of the House down to the 17th Edition, 1964) is 'the bible'. Basic procedure provides for full discussion both of general principles and details of Bills introduced, details usually being considered in smaller committees after the principles have been accepted by the House on 'Second Reading', (unlike some continental and American legislatures where Bills go first to committees.) Opportunities are provided for questions, debates on policy, and the airing of grievances. There is usually a Public Accounts Committee and an Estimates Committee and some Commonwealth countries make greater use of such specialized committees than Britain. Throughout the whole process, order in debate and the rights of minorities are preserved by Mr Speaker and it is interesting that some new Commonwealth countries have sought the services of British authorities in order to establish standards. For example, Sir Edward Fellowes, until recently Clerk to the House, was Speaker in the Nigerian House of Representatives for a time. Throughout the Commonwealth where parliamentary forms are maintained, the Speaker is expected to be impartial, though the tests of this are not always the same as in Britain. There, after being chosen, he ceases to be connected with a political party and is normally not opposed in his constituency. He never participates in debate and votes only to resolve a 'tie' and always so as to keep the matter open for further consideration. In some other Commonwealth countries he may, however, participate in debates when not in the

Chair. He may continue to be associated with a party and lose office when a party other than his own becomes the majority. This is not so in Britain, where the Labour Party has never yet provided a Speaker. In Canada it is a convention that French-speaking and English-speaking Canadians alternate in office and the Speaker has more than once been accused of partiality. Such minor deviations are now traditional and accepted in the countries concerned. But it is a mark either of the incipient breakdown of parliamentary forms or of their likely suppression when the Speaker can no longer control the House or ceases to be respected by it, just as it is when Oppositions refuse to debate and stage a 'walk-out'.

Members of legislatures are able to speak freely in the House because (again under normal conditions) they enjoy the privilege of absolute freedom of speech in debate and cannot be prosecuted for sedition or sued for libel or slander in respect of anything said during proceedings in the House. (That is why M.P.s are sometimes challenged to repeat their words outside the House!) In some countries where it may be desired to interfere with such freedom it is possible to remove such 'parliamentary immunity' or even to ignore it. Parliament is also able to protect itself from anyone who brings contempt on the proceedings of Parliament or who brings pressure to bear on members in the exercise of their duties. Again, a Parliament which seeks to protect itself against even fair criticism may abuse such rights to the detriment of the free expression of public opinion. We continually observe that the maintenance of parliamentary democracy is more than a matter of forms and rules; it depends essentially upon convention, political attitudes and, some would also argue, economic and social conditions.

The operation of a free Parliament depends directly upon free elections in which the electoral choice between contending parties is a real one. In most Commonwealth countries members of the Lower House are elected for single-member constituencies by an electorate based on universal suffrage (women may be excluded as, for example, in Northern Nigeria) and by voting by secret ballot, and anyone qualified to vote may offer himself as a candidate. Although names of candidates usually appear on a ballot paper (though not always their party—which is true of

Britain), in some countries ballot boxes are provided with different 'symbols' for the various parties so that illiterate voters are not confused, and, instead of a ballot paper a ball, for example, may be dropped in the appropriate box. Once more, in countries where the parliamentary spirit is not fully respected there may be "intimidation" of voters, personation, voting more than once, stuffing of ballot boxes with illegally obtained ballot papers marked in favour of a particular party, and many other devices. Candidates themselves may be intimidated and prevented from standing, or election meetings broken up. Bribery and corruption may exist. There may be valid explanations as to why these things occur and they may be no more than 'growing pains'. The British people have constantly to remember how long it took to establish their present form of government and that these practices are not confined to so-called 'under-developed' countries. But the practices themselves cannot be over-looked when we attempt to assess the future for effective parliamentary democracy in the Commonwealth.

The usual practice is for the candidate who gains the largest number of votes (even if he does not have an absolute majority i.e., more than half of all the votes cast) to be declared elected—what is popularly known in a typically English metaphor, as the 'first past the post' system. We need not go into the details of other systems. It is usually argued by the advocates of the system described that although it tends to exaggerate majorities in the Lower House (seats gained being more than proportionate to votes cast : indeed it is unusual for the winning party to obtain fifty per cent of the votes over the whole country—not even the Congress Party of India does this), and small parties (especially third parties) suffer, it does normally provide for effective one-party majorities in the legislature and hence to stable governments. In some countries this may be achieved by having large multi-member constituencies or even by taking the country as a whole as one constituency, putting up party lists, and giving all the seats to the party-list with a bare majority. This, of course, is another way of ensuring a one-party or one dominant-party system. It may, however, be quite unnecessary. In India, for example, the Congress Party as the party which achieved independence and which continued to be led for so long by Mr Nehru, was assured of an overwhelming majority in the Union Parliament on the 'first past the post' system (although not of a majority in every State election). The Tanganyika National Union, the Malawi Congress Party, the United Independence Party of Zambia, the Convention People's Party in Ghana before the establishment of a one-party state, were equally assured of an overwhelming majority without the assistance of a specially 'rigged' electoral system.

An attempt is usually made under the British type system to ensure reasonable equality of population as between constituencies though there are bound to be deviations from the mean, especially between the regular 'redistribution' of boundaries to meet shifts of population, and the size of constituencies will differ in different countries. In Britain the 'Standard' figure is 57,000, in New Zealand 15,000, in India anything between 500,000 and 750,000! The more sparsely populated a country is the larger must constituencies be to include the requisite number of voters; alternatively, as in Britain, rural constituencies will have a smaller number of electors than urban.

The right to vote is normally restricted to citizens of the country concerned under its own citizenship laws. The 'Commonwealth element' may be illustrated by the fact that in the United Kingdom, Canada, Australia (with certain exceptions) and New Zealand, British subjects or Commonwealth citizens (as defined in our section above on nationality) are entitled to vote, if they have qualified by residence, even though they are not citizens of that particular country. In this, their position is superior to that of aliens. In New Zealand, Maori electors vote in four separate Maori constituencies, but in no other independent Commonwealth country except Cyprus are there now such 'communal' constituencies. They are deemed to militate against national unity and to encourage separatism. The charge was often brought against the British that they used such devices e.g., in India in order to 'divide and rule'.

'Direct democracy', whereby electors may vote to 'recall' their representatives or can directly propose legislation ('the initiative') has not found favour in the British system of 'representative government'. Some use, however, has been made in the Commonwealth countries of the 'referendum', whereby people may vote directly to accept or reject Government or Parliamentary proposals. In Australia there must be a referendum on proposals to amend the Constitution. Referenda have been held in New Zealand on the question of prohibiting the sale of intoxicating liquors. In both Australia and New Zealand a referendum was held on the question of compulsory military service. Dr Nkrumah submitted his Republican Constitution in Ghana to a popular referendum. Where one party virtually controls the country the referendum is either unnecessary, or merely a method of publicly proving how popular the party and its proposals are. (In such circumstances even elections may merely be a nation-wide 'demonstration'.) There are, of course, the same possibilities of 'rigging' a referendum as those to which we referred in connection with elections.

We now look a little more closely at the place of Second Chambers (the 'Upper House') in Commonwealth constitutions. In federal systems, as we have seen, the Upper House is constructed so as to provide adequate representations for the units in the system. This is the case in Australia (with equal representation in the Senate elected by proportional representation in each State); Canada (with Senators appointed for life roughly in proportion to the population of the various regions, though on a party basis); India (where all but twelve of the members of the *Rajya Sabha* are elected by the State legislature); Malaysia (where two members each are elected by the State Legislatures and twenty-two are nominated by the Government); and Nigeria (where the Regional Legislatures i.e., virtually the Regional Governments, appoint the Senators, with smaller numbers representing the Mid-West Region and Lagos and four nominated by the Federal Government.) In Nigeria the Regional Upper Houses are Houses of Chiefs.

It is argued, for both Federal and Unitary systems, also, that there are other advantages in having a Second Chamber. Among unitary states in the Commonwealth, Britain, Ceylon, Jamaica and Trinidad have Second Chambers. Pakistan has never had one. Among the Commonwealth countries in Africa, apart from Nigeria, not one had a Second Chamber until Kenya (as part of the machinery to protect 'regional' interests) was provided with one in 1963. The 'orthodox' functions of a Second Chamber are to review and revise Bills (extremely useful when the Lower House is overburdened with work and legislation is often passed hastily); to initiate non-controversial Bills (including, sometimes, Government Bills); to debate general policy and—most controversial—to interpose delay. It was this last function, of course, which led to a reduction of the powers of the House of Lords, in 1911 and 1949. Delay has usually been imposed on so-called 'Radical' legislation proposed by so-called 'left-wing' governments, though it must be borne in mind that the House of Lords has been a predominantly hereditary body (though with some Life Peers since 1958) and therefore (or so it would be argued) essentially less 'progressive' and certainly less representative than a directly elected body. It must be mentioned, however, that it was a conservative government in New Zealand which abolished the Upper House (Legislative Council) in 1950 because it was controlled by the Labour Party! The argument in favour of a 'brake' is unlikely to be accepted by new and rapidly developing countries, particularly those dominated by one party. As Professor de Smith has aptly said, they 'will invariably seek to equip the legislative machine with a supercharger and overdrive in preference to disc brakes'.

Another argument which has been put forward in favour of an Upper House is that it provides an opportunity whereby a limited number of qualified persons, unable or unwilling to take part in the rough-and-tumble of party politics, can be associated with the process of government. Nomination is used for this purpose in India and Malaya, to a certain extent in Ceylon, but not in Canada. In some countries, for example, Nigeria, the Upper House is used as an appropriate place for traditional Chiefs. Second Chambers constituted in this way, however, can scarcely expect to be endowed with much power.

However constituted, in all countries in the Commonwealth (unlike the United States) the Upper House is much less influential than the Lower House, for it is on majority support in the latter that the Government relies for its retention of office, and it is usually only there that financial legislation can be originated or amended. Nevertheless, it is usual in Commonwealth countries for the Upper House to be able at least to delay all legislation— except financial. In Australia, Canada, and India, its passage may be prevented by the Upper House, deadlock being resolved in India by a joint sitting (in which, by sheer numbers the *Lok Sabha* will prevail); in Canada by the appointment of up to eight extra Senators (this might be insufficient but in practice the Senate never seeks a fight); in Australia, by a double dissolution of Parliament and elections to both Houses and, if still necessary, a joint sitting.

We note here the opinion expressed in the pamphlet already referred to at the beginning of this part.

'The possession of a parliament is not necessarily an indication of democratic government, and the term democracy has been so abused in recent times as almost to require definition. It is in an affirmative answer to the following questions that parliaments in the Commonwealth meet the test of democratic institutions. Is the parliament elected by the people through a secret ballot? Are elections held at frequent intervals? Do the people have a choice of candidates and programmes? Can any law-abiding citizen become a candidate? Does a minority have the right to become the majority by peaceful non-violent means? Is the Government responsible to the elected representatives?'

Clearly, not all Commonwealth countries, even those with a parliamentary as opposed to a presidential system could answer all these questions completely in the affirmative. We take up this point again later in more detail.

So far we have considered, for the most part, the electoral and parliamentary aspects of Commonwealth governments, though in passing we have referred to the executive. We must now examine the latter, and in particular the nature of the Cabinet system which, of course, distinguishes the British system from the Presidential system in at least three ways. First there is the separation of the Head of State (monarchical or republican) from the Head of Government. Secondly, there is the usual, though not inevitable rule that ministers are members of parliament and that there is no 'separation of powers' between executive and legislative. Thirdly, the executive is 'plural', despite the tendency for the powers of the Prime Minister to increase, not 'single'.

Constitutions and Governments

In effect the Cabinet is a committee of leading members of the majority party (or parties) in Parliament, although its members are chosen by the Prime Minister, himself the leader of the majority party, and not elected by the Legislature. Nor is it usual for the Prime Minister or for the Cabinet as a whole to have to seek prior approval of the legislature (as was, for a time, the practice in the Fourth French Republic and in some of the 'transitional' constitutions during the last stages of progress towards independence by British Colonies.[1]) Approval is shown by the acceptance of the Cabinet's proposals, and withdrawn by a vote of 'no confidence' on a specific issue.

In Britain the Cabinet and its functions are almost entirely a matter of 'convention'. In other Commonwealth countries these conventions—such as that the Head of State will call upon the leader who appears most likely to command a majority in the Lower House of Parliament to form a government; that the Head of State acts normally 'on advice' from the Cabinet; that the Cabinet will resign or request a dissolution if defeated on a matter which it regards as one of 'confidence', and many others—have been embodied in law. The most comprehensive statement of them is said to be contained in the Indian Constitution of 1950, though it appears that 'writing down' the conventions does not necessarily lead to greater certainty, since lawyers still disagree about the precise nature and limits of the powers of the Indian President!

The functions of the Cabinet have been described as follows :

1. The final determination of the policy to be submitted to Parliament :
2. The supreme control of the national executive in accordance with the policy agreed by Parliament :
3. The continuous co-ordination and delimitation of the authority of the several Departments of State.

But the Cabinet is essentially a political body. It depends for its continued existence upon the support of a majority in an elected legislature and must be constantly concerned with the 'art of management' of its majority. It must further remember that in not longer than the specified time (five years in Britain,

[1] On this, see the author's *The Cabinet in the Commonwealth*, Stevens, 1958.

89

for example), if not sooner, it will have to 'go to the country' and seek approval of its past policies and record and a 'mandate' for its future programme. Of course, in circumstances where the party is assured of electoral victory, by whatever means, this last factor is less important. Nor is the art of management so subtle where expulsion from the party through disagreement may be the end of the offending member's political life.

Indeed, so bound up with the party system is the Cabinet system that it was not until the emergence of modern political parties in the nineteenth century that the British Cabinet assumed its present form. It now consists of Members of Parliament with the same or similar political views and chosen from the party (or parties in the case of the—now rare-coalition) having a majority in the elected House of the legislature. There is also a common responsibility signified by collective resignation in the event of parliamentary censure on a major issue (though individual ministers may accept personal responsibility and resign without bringing down the Government; or the Government may rally round a criticized Minister and protect him by its majority; or he may be transferred to another post, with or without temporary resignation.) A common leadership is acknowledged in the Prime Minister who has, in Britain, become increasingly powerful in recent years and is able, within certain political limits, to select and change his Ministers and exercise those 'hire and fire powers' implied in Mr Gladstone's remark that every Prime Minister should be 'a good butcher'. Such power is not unknown in other Commonwealth countries (even when it has not led to the formal establishment of a Presidential system), from India, with the undoubted eminence for so many years of Mr Nehru, to Malawi, where Dr Hastings Banda has been able to get rid of half a dozen colleagues without, apparently, his own position being affected. On the other hand, Ceylon provides an example of a country where soon after independence the Prime Minister felt it necessary to circulate a memorandum to his colleagues reminding them, for example, of the convention of 'collective responsibility' and that they should not attack Government policy or the policy of other Ministers in public! More recently, Mrs Bandaranaike has found her authority undermined by inability to keep even a small majority, though this is related to the fluidity of the party system. Breaches of collective responsibility have not been unknown even in the 'older Dominions'.

Different political conditions have, of course, necessarily brought about variations in Cabinet practice. This is particularly true of federal systems. In these the Cabinet has proved to be at least as important as the Second Chamber for the protection of regional interests. All six Australian States are normally represented in the Cabinet. In Canada it is the practice for Ministers to be so chosen that the several regions are fairly balanced in the federal Cabinet and where if a proposal adversely affects one region it is possible for the Minister representing that region virtually to interpose a veto. There is always an equal number of Ministers from Quebec and Ontario and each of the other provinces is usually represented by at least one Minister. In India the various States, regions, religious and other interests must somehow be reconciled by access to the supreme centre of power, the Cabinet. All this, of course, is made easier where nation-wide parties exist, so that a one-party Cabinet can contain representatives of all the major interests. It has sometimes been difficult for the majority party in Canada to find men from each province of sufficient calibre for Cabinet status, as is also true in regard to the smaller States of Australia. Men of less ability have to be included to preserve the regional balance. This may be so even in unitary states where different shades of opinion must be catered for, but it is a far more serious problem in federations. Nigeria provides perhaps an extreme example of the problem. Each of the three original main parties drew its strength from one Region; there were no nation wide parties. No one party, therefore, included suitable ministerial candidates from all three Regions. From 1960 to 1964 the Western Region was excluded from the Cabinet; its Action Group Party was in opposition. The split of 1962 in the West produced the Nigerian National Democratic Party, which became allied with the Northern People's Party. But in 1964 the (Eastern) National Council of Nigerian Citizens broke with its Northern allies and it appeared that the East would cease to be represented in the Government after the Elections. The Action Group also would be excluded, and many people felt that the N.N.D.P. was unrepresentative of the West.

91

It may be added that in multi-racial societies the Cabinet can be used to associate the various groups with government. This has been the case in India, Ceylon (until recently with the exclusion of the Tamils) and Malaysia. Where, however, the division is between Whites and Blacks, as for example, in Kenya or Northern Rhodesia (Zambia) a multi-racial Cabinet may be wholly artificial in that no multi-racial party is able to win an election, and a white minority which controls the Government will include only 'cooperative' Africans (described by the nationalist leaders as 'stooges' or 'Uncle Toms') who are unrepresentative. When African Governments succeed to power in such societies, they may include Europeans, but only on merit and subject to political compatibility, not as 'selected representatives'.

We have said that in the normal pattern of Cabinet Government, which prevails in Britain and in most other Commonwealth countries, Ministers are at liberty to speak and vote only in the House of which they are members. In India and Malaysia, however, they may speak in either House, though they may vote only in the House of which they are members. (As a matter of interest, in some countries Ministers cease to be members of either House when appointed, though they may speak in them. This is true of France, where, however, the system is in practice more presidential than parliamentary.)

A Prime Minister when forming his Cabinet must take into consideration, in addition to the political and regional factors described above, the question of the size of the Cabinet. In Britain the practice now is to differentiate between Ministers who are full members of the Cabinet and those who, though of Cabinet rank (above Junior Ministers) only attend meetings when matters concerning their departments are under discussion. In this way the size of British Cabinets has been kept at an average of between sixteen and twenty (though the Labour Government of 1964 included twenty-three Ministers in the Cabinet.) There are at least as many (again excluding Junior Ministers) outside. Some other Commonwealth countries follow the same practice. In India there are usually twelve members in the Cabinet with some fourteen 'Ministers of State', as well as about twenty 'Deputy Ministers', outside it. In 1956 Australia adopted this pattern for the first time, establishing a Cabinet of twelve with ten others outside. It will be noted that Cabinets may be smaller in federal countries since the functions of government are divided between the centre and the units. In other Commonwealth countries the Cabinet has continued to include all the principle Ministers (though Junior Ministers and Parliamentary Secretaries remain outside); indeed, Ministers sometimes hold more than one portfolio i.e., are responsible for more than one department. The Prime Minister may also take responsibility for a department e.g., the Foreign Office, but this is increasingly difficult because of the enormous expansion of the scope of government for which he has overall responsibility.

This same expansion has also everywhere made more difficult the task of coordination. In many countries this function of the Cabinet has been assisted by the establishment of a Secretariat of permanent officials, primarily as a recording and informing agency. For a long time in Britain it was feared that the keeping of Cabinet records and the presence of officials would endanger the principle of cabinet secrecy which is essential if collective responsibility is to be maintained in public, while at the same time differences of opinion may be discussed in private. Now, however, the necessity of a Secretariat is firmly recognized; it may even include economic and statistical sections. It is of great assistance especially to the Prime Minister, although in some countries there is also a Prime Minister's Office. A Cabinet Secretariat was established in Australia in 1939 and in Canada in 1940. The terms of reference of the latter provide a good description of the work performed. They were : to prepare, under the direction of the Prime Minister, the agenda for Cabinet meetings; to keep records of such meetings; to prepare in advance information necessary for Cabinet deliberations; to communicate Cabinet decisions to Ministers and others concerned; and to maintain liaison between the Cabinet and its committees.

Such committees have become increasingly necessary as a means of improving administrative coordination and also of allowing for a degree of specialization (though in some countries, especially federal, their use has been limited because they cannot be as fully representative of all interests as the Cabinet itself and therefore the latter has to duplicate committee discussions). Committees provide an opportunity for ministerial heads of departments, including those not in the Cabinet, to discuss matters with which their own departments are concerned before they reach the Cabinet either as agreed recommendations which are often accepted by the Cabinet with little or no discussion (particularly if the Committee has been chaired by a high-ranking Cabinet Minister who may have been given special responsibility for the field of administration concerned), or else as clearly formulated issues for final Cabinet decision. It is not possible to describe in detail the arrangement of Cabinet Committees in current operation in any country because knowledge of this would infringe the principle of secrecy of deliberations necessary to preserve ultimate collective responsibility. But it is certain that most Cabinets will establish committees in such fields as defence and foreign policy as well as either continuing or *ad hoc* committees in a large variety of other fields.

It is probable that in most Cabinets, however small, there develops a sort of 'Inner Cabinet' consisting of the Prime Minister and those colleagues with whom he is particularly intimate or whom he most trusts. The relations between a Prime Minister and his colleagues will depend to a great extent on his own personality and wishes. But many Prime Ministers may exercise as much power, at least in certain critical circumstances, as many Presidents who are technically individually responsible rather than having to ensure 'collective responsibility'.

Nothing is more certain than that the 'political executive' cannot itself conduct all the affairs of a vast state; indeed, even at the highest levels the politicians will need advice from permanent officials, unless their party organization is such that it can both obtain and keep a virtual monopoly of expertise and 'non-political' wisdom (which will generally mean that the civil service itself becomes politicized.) It is of the essence of parliamentary goverment on the British model that below the political level (which goes no further down than the junior ministers and parliamentary secretaries) officials should retain their posts irrespective of changes of government—a 'merit' not a 'spoils' system. Such a system was only gradually established in Britain from the middle of the nineteenth century onwards (while in the United States it took longer to develop, is by no means universally accepted, especially in the separate States, and even at federal level does not go so far *up* the scale as in Britain). These historical facts must never be overlooked when an attempt is made to assess the 'failure' (or the deliberate refusal) of some Commonwealth countries to maintain the same kind of non-political civil service as in Britain.

The British system implies that the public service should be open to all citizens on the basis of merit (though the charge that conditions of entry were for long such that only those with a certain educational and social background could hope to enter the highest grade was—and is—frequently made.) More important perhaps, is the firm convention that the task of the civil service should not be to formulate policy but to advise the Government of the day and implement the policy approved by the legislature (though it is obvious that top-level civil servants do, in fact, influence policy albeit the Minister has the last word). The politician, subject to parliamentary approval, takes responsibility for the consequences of policy and administration.

All this further implies that regardless of changes in the party or parties which compose the government of the day, senior civil servants should not engage in day-to-day political activity. Every civil servant remains free to express his political views through the ballot box (which, of course, demands that it must be inviolably secret), but active participation in the political arena is considered liable to affect the civil servant's impartial loyalty to his political superiors and endanger the picture of him in the public eye as political neutral. The lower branches of the public service are allowed complete or considerable political activity (though there are frequent arguments about where to draw the line between the grades and between different types and levels of political activity); but strict limits are set to such activity by more senior officers. Indeed the latter are expected to remain 'anonymous' so far as the general public is concerned, though this is very difficult in smaller countries, increasingly difficult even in 'advanced' countries owing to the publicity given to senior advisers, and probably impossible where there are disagreements between nationalist ministers and 'expatriate' civil servants.

To ensure the maintenance of 'British standards' as far as possible, Commonwealth countries have usually maintained the Public Service Commission established during the transition to independence; its function is to ensure impartiality in the selection of candidates for recruitment and in many cases (though not so with the Civil Service Commission in Britain) to supervise to some extent at least promotion, discipline and possibly salaries and conditions of service. But, as we shall see, changes in the status of the Public Service Commission are frequently made soon after independence.

Indeed, all these aspects of political neutrality and insulation from political influence have not been so strictly observed even in the 'older Dominions'. In many newer Commonwealth members there has been an even sharper variation from the standards laid down during the period of dependence and—usually —reasserted immediately afterwards. Even in India, with a well-established *Indian* civil service (though one brought up in the British tradition) politicians and civil servants have not always seen eye to eye. 'Political' transfers have been made. Many functions have been handed over to public corporations and other 'quasi-government bodies' where civil service standards do not prevail. In many other countries nationalist politicians newly come to power did not always feel that their 'expatriate' civil servants were in sympathy with either their political aims or methods, a feeling which was sometimes justified. But the process of 'nativization' of the civil service could be pursued only so far if breakdown was not to be risked.

Yet, at the top level, Ministers felt the need of advisers who understood them and shared their purposes and, short of the French system of introducing a small group to form 'a minister's cabinet' and to strengthen his hand against the permanent civil service (a remedy which has even been suggested in Britain), the only way was to recruit people known to be politically in line with the ruling politicans. For regional or local government politicians were often appointed in place of the old 'neutral' District Officers to ensure that government policies were carried out. Ghana and Tanganyika afford examples of this. Moreover, during the struggle for independence civil servants had frequently played an active part in politics *either* within the nationalist movement *or* in collaboration with the Colonial Administration. In the latter cases the politicans could feel no confidence in them; in the former they expected their due reward.

Constitutions and Governments

Nor is there such a wealth of talent in some countries that able men can be 'artifically' kept out of politics, (which may end in their being excluded from governmental decisions altogether) or, if involved in politics, barred from important administrative functions. More generally, just as 'opposition' comes to be regarded as almost treasonable in view of the immense tasks facing governments who seek both national unity and social and economic modernization at the same time, so 'neutrality' is interpreted as a sign of less than the desired enthusiasm for the new aims and purposes of government. Yet another factor affects recruitment. In countries divided regionally, ethnically, or by caste, the various sections have to be persuaded to support the government. There were insufficient political jobs to go round. Civil service jobs, or jobs on the various boards, corporations or commissions have to be used. All this is quite apart from the demands of the different sections for 'fair' representation in the public services and which led for example to 'reserved' places in India for members of various castes including the 'Scheduled Castes'—the 'untouchables'.

Once again these factors are discussed to explain and not to attempt to justify these 'deviations' from what might be called the 'Whitehall model'. Nor is it suggested that there might not eventually be changes, as, indeed, there have been in Britain and the United States and, even more recently, in some of the 'older Dominions'.

One feature of parliamentary democracy which is stressed by those who regard it as the best form of government is the existence of what is called 'the rule of law'. Control over the Government is primarily exercized through the political responsibility of Ministers to Parliament to the electorate. But 'free government' demands the further subordination to the 'rule of law'. This implies that power is not arbitrarily used, that no one is above the law, that all are equal before it, that no one can be convicted of a crime except as against the laws of the State previously enacted by Parliament; that an accused person is assumed to be innocent until proved guilty by an established court in which he may call witnesses in his own defence; and that all may seek redress for wrongs suffered. This is an idealized description to which many reservations and modifications would have to be made in describing any actual system of government in practice. The details are too technical for discussion here. But parliamentary democracy is said to require as near an approach to these ideals as possible and a constant striving towards them.

Most fundamental to the rule of law is the independence of the judiciary of control by either the executive or the electorate and even safeguards against ill-considered action by the legislature. This requires that members of the judiciary, although appointed by the Government in the first place, enjoy a tenure of office that is thereafter completely independent of the Government. Judges are appointed from outstanding members of the legal profession, and are normally given a high salary both to emphasise the responsibilities of their office and to place them beyond the reach of financial influence. All this, again, applies fully only to the higher judges and, in some Commonwealth countries, not fully to them. We consider this further in our account of specific countries. First, however, there is one significant new departure related to the rule of law which deserves separate consideration.

IV : BILLS OF RIGHTS IN THE COMMONWEALTH

Following the views of Professor A.V. Dicey in his *Law of the Constitution,* it is generally held in Britain that the fundamental freedoms such as freedom of speech, freedom of religion, freedom from arbitrary arrest, freedom of peaceful assembly, are better secured by the ordinary remedies of the law, administered by impartial judges. This has not been accepted in many continental countries nor in the United States. One of the most interesting features of many new Commonwealth countries is the inclusion of an elaborate Bill of Rights to guarantee such freedoms. One reason for this has been a growing doubt whether the 'rule of law' can, in all circumstances, be best guaranteed in the British manner, or whether some further safeguard is not desirable. We shall preface our study of particular constitutions by an examination of Bills of Rights in Commonwealth countries and then examine the extent to which the rule of law, with or without such additional protection is, in fact, maintained. Here is perhaps the most serious test of how far members of the Commonwealth still speak a 'common political idiom' and share the same philosophy of government.

Before turning specifically to Bills of Rights we look briefly at other safeguards which have been inserted into constitutions in the hope that they might prevent abuse of majority power. We have already noted that all Commonwealth countries except Britain have a written constitution in the technical sense. One safeguard is that such constitution cannot normally be altered except by some special procedure requiring more than a bare majority vote in the legislature, while the courts usually have jurisdiction to pronounce a measure void if it is repugnant to the constitution. In some cases the device of the referendum may be used.

Secondly, the electoral system and the allocation of seats in the legislature may be so devised as to assure members of minority groups that their voices will be heard. But, as we have seen, communal electorates for this purpose are now frowned upon.

Thirdly, and this too we have already discussed, it is possible to guarantee special representation for minority and regional interests and traditional elements in a Second Chamber. The Second Chamber may also be required to cooperate in the amendment of the Constitution, thus making this more difficult. (The first and third safeguards may be eroded by political developments. For instance in Kenya certain parts of the constitution could be amended only by a seventy-five per cent majority in the Lower House and a ninety per cent majority in the Upper House; President Kenyatta's Kenya African National Union was able to achieve these majorities.)

Fourthly there may be a special constitutional mechanism designed to obstruct the enactment of legislation that discriminates against communal groups, though this is more evident during the stage of dependency, when the Governor may be required to 'reserve' such legislation. Majority parties, on winning independence, are reluctant to accept such restrictions. Kenya and Malawi, among others, rejected such mechanisms, while in Malaysia there is a curious reversal of the normal position since the 'special position' of the Malays, the largest community, is in certain ways entrenched in the constitution.

Fifthly, attempts may be made to 'screen certain sensitive areas of public administration from political control' : the delimitation of electoral constituencies (as through the Boundary Commission in Britain); the conduct of elections (though it is significant that certain members of the Electoral Commission in Nigeria resigned in 1964 because they were not satisfied with the way in which elections were being conducted); the administration of justice; the process of prosecution (though in several cases this has now become a political matter where 'State' offences are involved); the civil service and police (though we have already noted the tendency to 'politicize' the civil service); the audit of public accounts.

Sixthly, the status and dignity of traditional rulers may be expressly safeguarded against derogation at the hands of the majority in the legislature, though in many cases the Chiefs are rendered harmless by relegation to a Second Chamber or are deprived of political influence unless it is clearly exercized in favour of the majority party.

Seventhly, as we have seen there may be division of legislature and executive powers either by means of a federal constitution or by the establishment of strong regions. The latter, however, is seldom permanent. In both Ghana and Kenya regional safeguards were whittled away or rendered innocuous by extended party supervision and control.

Finally, we turn to the question of Bills of Rights. As we stated above, British legal opinion has not favoured the idea of such Bills. India's Republican Constitution of 1950 included a set of 'fundamental rights' (as did Pakistan's abortive constitution of 1956) and in 1957 the Federation of Malaya followed suit. But the former constitution was home-made and the latter derived from the recommendations of a Commission which included Australian, Indian and Pakistani members. However, there then followed the change of attitude in Britain itself. In 1959 a list of fundamental rights was incorporated in the Nigerian Constitution ('made in Britain', though with consultations with Nigerian leaders). Then Her Majesty's Government itself expressed its 'firm view' that legal provisions were 'needed' in the proposed new Constitution of Kenya 'for the judicial protection of human rights'. The Monckton Commission had already recommended constitutional Bills of Rights for the (then) Federation of Rhodesia and Nyasaland and its three territories. By the end of 1962 Nigeria, Sierra Leone, Jamaica, Trinidad and Tobago, Uganda, Kenya, Southern Rhodesia, Malta, British Guiana and Aden all had constitutional Bills of Rights. Cyprus had already acquired her own. More significantly, Canada, of the 'older Dominions' had joined the group.

Certain guarantees, it is true, had earlier been incorporated in the Canadian Constitution—for example, protection of certain denominational schools and the equality of the English and French languages for specified purposes. The Australian Constitution laid down, for example, that the acquisition of property by the Federal Government had to be on 'just terms', that freedom of movement between the States and the free exercise of religion be guaranteed. A few constitutions for dependent territories also contained certain guarantees, for example against discrimination on grounds of race or religion. But it would seem that Nigeria really set the example, primarily because of political rivalries on a regional basis and the fears of minorities. Guarantees were intended as a substitute for the creation of new regions based on minorities. Individual rights were protected rather than the entrenchment of minority rights as such. The basis of the guarantees was the assertion of liberties and immunities or fundamental freedoms on the one hand, and safeguards for fair procedure in civil and criminal proceedings on the other. Furthermore, any law inconsistent with the Bill of Rights is void to the extent of the inconsistency. The Courts are the interpreters of such issues. It must be noted, however, that it remained possible for the Federal Government to declare a state of emergency. This happened with respect to the Western Region in 1962 when preventive detention or restriction of political opponents and security suspects became legal, though an advisory tribunal was established to which detainees might have their case referred.

It would be tedious to examine in similar detail the Bills of Rights subsequently established, largely on the Nigerian model, though with some variations. In each case the guarantees are entrenched and cannot be amended or repealed except by a special procedure. However, there is some evidence that Bills of Rights offer no more guarantee of the 'rule of law' than other types of safeguards, particularly in times of crisis when they are most needed. Under Presidential rule in Pakistan the fundamental rights are not justiciable, i.e. they cannot be the subject of action in the courts. In Southern Rhodesia protection has not prevented legislation which even the Chief Justice declared to be against the rule of law and under which African leaders are restricted. The actions taken against the opposition in Ghana and perhaps also those in the Western Region of Nigeria (although such men as Chief Awolowo and Chief Enahoro appear to have been fairly charged and duly convicted) suggest the fragile nature of any protections, since of the two latter examples the second had a Bill of Rights, the first only Dicey's guarantee of the 'ordinary law of the land'.

Too often is it legal for Ministers to find a way round guarantees if they deem it necessary on a number of prescribed grounds, (though in some cases the judges need not necessarily accept a ministerial certificate of such grounds). It is worth noting that the Canadian Bill of Rights is not a constitutional amendment and therefore, can be amended or repealed by the Federal Parliament by the ordinary legislative process. But it is doubtful whether this signifies any less respect for the freedoms guaranteed. We thus come back to the point that there may be something in the suggestion that Bills of Rights exist mainly where threats to freedom are greatest but that they may, in fact, provide inadequate protection because the existence of such threats is often used to justify temporary or partial abrogation of such Bills.

To sum up, it appears that traditional British prejudices against Bills of Rights rapidly disappeared largely because of the evidence that majority political parties in new states could seldom be persuaded to accept more conspicuous guarantees for minority interests. They are so formulated as to appear to protect individual liberties and thus the rule of law rather than group interests as such. Yet, as the experience of the United States shows, they can serve indirectly as a valuable instrument for sustaining the interests of minority groups and lend potent support to the principles of constitutional government. But these results only come about if the judges are able to resist encroachment on the guarantees provided and this is not always as possible in some of the newer Commonwealth countries as in the United States. Even in India, where the Government has committed itself to the principles of parliamentary democracy and judicial independence, unwelcome judicial interpretations of the guarantees of fundamental rights have provoked rapid constitutional amendments, notably in respect of 'adequate compensation' for property compulsorily acquired. In 1965 the Indian Government deemed it necessary to arrest hundreds of 'Pekin-orientated' Communists under preventive detention legislation such as provoked anti-British campaigns in many dependent territories before 1945. It may justifiably be argued that 'the country in danger' justifies such action; but the question nevertheless remains 'who next?' South Africa has extended the definition of 'Communist' to include almost anyone who is to the slightest extent critical of the Government.

Finally, it must be said that in a one-party state where organized dissent is regarded as sedition, justiciable guarantees of freedom 'can hardly be more than empty shells'. Ghana and Tanganyika have no Bill of Rights. In the former even the few guarantees in the Constitution of 1957 have been removed. In the latter an African spokesman declared that a Bill of Rights merely invites conflict between the executive and the judiciary! In neither country is the judiciary really a major independent force in the governmental process. Pakistan too, has dispensed with justiciable guarantees. 'There is close correlation between allegiance to the general principles of constitutionalism and readiness to accept and abide by a justiciable constitutional Bill of Rights.'[1]

The opinion might even be ventured that a Bill of Rights presupposes such a high level of constitutional morality that, if it existed, no Bill would be necessary. On the other hand, such Bills at least keep alive standards of just government and are both a goad to the consciences of those who ignore them and a guide to those who hope that they may one day be effective.

V : FEDERALISM IN THE COMMONWEALTH

Any account of constitutions in the Commonwealth must look at, however briefly, the federal systems. There were two, Australia

[1]Prof. S.A. de Smith. *op. cit.* Cha. V. on which most of this section relies.

and Canada, among the 'older Dominions'; among the new are India, Malaysia and Nigeria, while Pakistan retains some federal features and Uganda is part-federation (five important areas, pre-eminently Buganda, enjoying federal relations with the central government). The original independence constitution of Kenya had such large elements of entrenched regionalism in it as to be federal in everything but name, though most of these elements were subsequently removed and, in any case, rendered virtually nugatory when the opposition party, the Kenya African Democratic Union, merged with the majority Kenya African National Union. It is, of course, impossible to describe each of these systems in detail, but some general points are worth examination. Most of them concern the newer Commonwealth countries.

India and Nigeria, as large, diverse, multi-lingual countries, naturally resistant to uniformity in government and administration, inevitably established federal systems. Pakistan had to accept some degree of federalization in view of the geographical separation of East Bengal from the rest of the country and the linguistic and cultural differences between East and West. In Malaya, an attempt to introduce a unitary system after World War II met with opposition; the existence of traditional rulers and institutions made some form of federalism inevitable. The federal form, of course, made the adhesion of Singapore, British Borneo (Sabah) and Sarawak, (though not yet Brunei) possible. Malaysia is a somewhat looser federation than Malaya had been. In Uganda the federal principle was conceded reluctantly as the only means of keeping Buganda within the new independent unit. (The South Arabian Federation, not yet independent, may, it appears from pronouncements of the Colonial Secretary at the end of 1964, achieve independence as a unitary state.) Space prevents consideration of the break-up of the West Indian Federation.

Nigeria and Uganda are clearly identifiable federations with multi-party parliamentary systems, though in the former, one party dominates each Region, while in the latter in 1964 several members of the Democratic Party crossed the floor to join the Uganda National Congress and a one-party system may yet emerge, since many supporters of the Buganda party, the Kabaka Yekka, have already joined the Congress. Each represents a federation which was created out of a virtually unitary system in response to pressure from below. This urge to federalism may be significant in relation to ideas for the creation of wider federations among African States : if unitary states have to be converted into federations the prospect of creating new federations by joining together existing unitary states must appear remote. The most promising possibility, that of an East African Federation to include Tanganyika, Uganda and Kenya seems unlikely to materialize in the near future and it is still too early to say precisely how the 'union' of Tanganyika and Zanzibar to form Tanzania will operate. Moreover, the widespread trend towards the elimination of organized opposition in new African States raises the question not merely of whether further federations can be formed—particularly if they involved joining together democratic and authoritarian, or even two one-party states, but also of the future of existing federal states. Even the future of Nigeria remains uncertain; there was talk of secession by the Eastern Region after the 1964 elections and some elements at least in the North would appear to regard this possibility as not altogether undesirable. We cannot, however, rule out the emergence of new kinds of association between African States, though a discussion of the form these might take would carry us too far afield.

The most obvious feature of the new Commonwealth federations is the dominance of the central authority. Federal legislative and executive powers are ample to coerce recalcitrant regional governments and there is the financial superiority of the Centre. The predominance of the Centre in Malaysia will be modified by the inclusion of Singapore, but 'confrontation' with Indonesia seems likely to increase central powers the longer it persists. In India, the dangers of provincialism (emphasized by the early demand for linguistic states) and the need for national planning of economic development and social welfare, as well as the predominance of Congress and of Mr Nehru, produced important centralizing features in the constitution and a great deal of centralization in practice. The President has more than once established 'President's rule' in some States. In Nigeria the powers of the Centre were amply illustrated by the action taken in the Western Region in 1962 when for some time the Region was governed by a Federal Administrator.

None of these new federations is an aggregation of formerly *independent* states and the principal 'founding fathers' were nationalists concerned to prevent disunity and foster rapid economic development and social change. On the other hand the power of the Regions, particularly in Northern Nigeria, is clear and it may be that the North would prefer secession to a federation in which it did not have a predominant voice. In India, centrifugal forces remain strong and it may be that Mr Shastri will be less able to preserve centralized control—or less wishful to do so—than Mr Nehru.

Far more detail is included in the new federal constitutions than in the old. Legislative lists, federal and provincial, are longer and the list of 'concurrent powers' clearly provides for an extension of central influence and control. Regional interests may be entrenched in far more detail. Yet in case of inconsistency federal laws prevail over provincial. Provision is made for the inter-delegation of legislative and executive powers between the Centre and the units, though in some cases this is possible only *from* a unit *to* the Centre. The Centre may be empowered to legislate to ensure uniformity in certain fields and may be given coercive powers to prevent a unit from seriously obstructing the working of the federal scheme of government. India is the main example here. All the constitutions confer emergency powers on the Centre.

In general, the federal principle is realized more fully in Nigeria than elsewhere. The Centre has no direct control in normal circumstances over regional governments or legislatures and no voice in appointments to the regional judiciary or public service. The Regions are represented on the Federal Supreme Court and the Electoral Commission (though, as we have seen, this did not preclude disputes in 1964) and the regional constitutions cannot be changed by the Federal Parliament though, conversely, the Regions cannot themselves make major amendments without Federal approval. Most important amendments to the Federal Constitution require regional participation. Legislative powers reserved to the Regions are considerable and they are guaranteed certain financial resources to carry out their functions.

Some of these features appear in the other federal constitutions though none appear in them all. In Pakistan the subordination of the provinces is strongly emphasized and presidential authority is very pronounced. In India, State Bills may be reserved for presidential consideration, judicial appointments are made by the Centre, State constitutions can be amended by the Union (Federal) Parliament and State participation in the amending process for the Federal Constitution is limited to a small number of matters. In Malaya, the constitution was virtually quasi-unitary, although there is more decentralization under the constitution of Malaysia. As in all federations, cooperative devices to channel federal aid to the units disguise the ultimate power of the Centre, while borrowing for large-scale development is also centralized.

Clearly, federalism cannot continue to exist unless the dominant political forces acquiesce in the observance of rules determining the limits of governmental authority. In most of the new states not only political but economic factors are likely to cause the balance of power to tilt more and more towards the Centre. Yet federalism still has a strong appeal as a constitutional safeguard for regional minorities and may be regarded as supplementing the guarantee of individual freedoms by Bills of Rights. There have been times when federalism appeared to be likely to give way to a more unitary system under the stress of war and economic crisis—though Western Australia at one time thought of secession. In Canada the threat to federalism is posed by the separatists in Quebec who appeared stronger than ever in 1964. Yet both systems, it may be suggested, are likely to persist. The same is likely to be true certainly of India and probably of Malaysia (subject to whatever may occur if the threat from Indonesia is extended). In Nigeria the future is obviously one either of continued federation (possibly with the creation of additional regions) or break-up, certainly not a unitary form of government.

If we are looking for evidence that some ideals are still shared in common at least by a large proportion of Commonwealth countries, it is clear that the maintenance of federal systems, with some distribution of powers and hence greater guarantees of individual and minority rights, is one way of keeping open the possibility of realizing these ideals in practice.[1]

---

[1] I am again indebted in this section to Prof. S.A. de Smith, *op. cit.*

VI : PRESIDENTIAL AND REPUBLICAN SYSTEMS

Any attempt to pick out significant constitutional variations in the Commonwealth must clearly have regard to the emergence of Presidential systems as perhaps marking the greatest deviation from the Westminster model. Republics which, like India, preserve the parliamentary system and merely replace an hereditary 'ceremonial' Monarch by an elected 'ceremonial' President are not fundamentally very far removed from the British system *merely* because of this change. But where the President is at once the ceremonial and effective Head, something approaching either the American or the French (Fifth Republic) model has come into being. We shall look at three such regimes, Pakistan, Ghana and Tanganyika, for further illustrations of this general point.

Pakistan came into being as a result of the partition of the Indian sub-continent under the leadership of Mohamed Ali Jinnah (whose sister contested the Presidential election against President Ayub in 1965). He became Governor-General, President of the Constituent Assembly and chairman at Cabinet meetings. He was succeeded by the Prime Minister, Liaquat Ali Khan, who, despite his undoubted ability and prestige, was able to make little headway with the solution of his country's problems before his assassination in 1951. In the next seven years Pakistan had six Prime Ministers and may more provincial Chief Ministers. The Centre continually interfered in provincial affairs. Meanwhile, the first 'Constituent Assembly' was dissolved in 1954 without having provided an acceptable constitution and the second produced a republican constitution in 1956 which was abrogated in 1958 without ever having been brought into successful operation. From 1958 to 1962 the country was under martial law. In the latter year the new presidential constitution again came under stress. Throughout the whole period innumerable political groups failed to tackle the country's problems, the public service was breaking down and an economic crisis was always around the corner.

President Ayub Khan, who has always described himself as 'a reluctant politician', was determined 'to restore democracy but of the type that people can understand and work'. This he has sought to do by the establishment of 'basic democracies'. At the lowest level these comprise the directly elected urban councils and the partly-elective village councils. Above them come sub-divisional, district, divisional and finally provincial councils. All councils, except at the lowest levels, include a substantial appointed element. In 1960 the Basic Democracies, making up 80,000 members, were elected. They immediately gave a vote of confidence (95.6 per cent) to the President; there were no other candidates. The President then established a constitutional commission but to his dismay there were strong demands for a return to parliamentary government. The commission's draft proposals of 1961 suggested that the President should select his own Cabinet and govern independently of the legislature. But the latter would have power to override the President by a two-thirds majority and would control the Budget. Members would be directly elected, though an interim legislature would be created by the votes of the 'Basic Democrats'. Pakistan would continue to be federal, with two provincial legislatures. The constitution promulgated on 1 March, 1962, made some concessions to these views (especially in accepting federalism) but it reflected the President's determination to create a strong, stable system of government. Some of his comments are worthy of quotation :

'We have adopted the Presidential system as it is simpler to work, more akin to our genius and history, and less liable to lead to instability—a luxury that a developing country like ours cannot afford. The other alternative was the Parliamentary system. This we tried, and it failed. Not that there is anything inherently wrong with it. The trouble is that we have not attained several sophistications that are necessary for its successful operation. . . . Above all, you really need[a] cool and phlegmatic temperament, which only people living in cold climates seem to have. Also it requires [a] long period of probation. For instance, the British took six hundred years of trial and tribulation to reach this stage. . . . So don't let us kid ourselves and cling to clichés and assume that we are ready to work such a refined system knowing the failure of earlier attempts.'

This is an excellent summary of the various factors which many people consider go far to explain deviations from the Westminster model, and one given by a Pakistani who was obviously sincere. Other deviations in other countries, though perhaps due to many of the same causes, have occurred not to the regret of those responsible but with obvious intent, and with little or no *ex post facto* attempt at justification.

Certainly the most obvious feature of Pakistan's new constitution was the concentration of power in the hands of the President. All executive authority is vested in the office of the President. He appoints the commanders of the armed forces, the Governors of the Provinces, the Ministers of the Central Government and their parliamentary secretaries, as well as the Chief Justice. There is no Prime Minister. The President can issue ordinances, valid for six months. He may refer any dispute between himself and the Assembly to a referendum of the members of the Basic Democracies. He may dissolve the Assembly at any time, and this is followed by a general election *and* a presidential election. He is elected by the Basic Democrats and is eligible for two five-year terms in office. (In 1965 President Ayub defeated his only opponent, Miss Jinnah, by a majority of between two and three to one, and began his second term of office.) The President may be impeached by the Assembly but only on a three-quarters majority of its total membership.

In the National Assembly the two Provinces have been given equal representation; members are elected by the Basic Democrats. In the elections of 1962 candidates were forbidden to present themselves as members of, or supported by political parties. But the electoral college none-the-less chose a considerable number of familiar political figures and the new Assembly immediately began to agitate for a relaxation of the ban on political parties. The ban was removed, with certain exceptions, in July, 1962 and at once parties, new and old, began to proliferate. Within six months the Government's majority in the Assembly became precarious, while provincial rivalries again appeared. The President felt that he too must seek the backing of a party and in May, 1963, he joined one which put itself forward as the legitimate successor to the Muslim League, under which Pakistan had won independence. By 1963 it appeared that this new regime might be well-established, despite the continued demand for a parliamentary system and charges that the presidential election was 'rigged'. Much, however, will depend on the elections to the legislatures which had not, at the time of writing, (Jan. 1965) been held.

There are some other features of the constitution which must be noted if we are to judge how far Pakistan has departed not merely from the parliamentary model but from the general 'rule of law'. Firstly, though this is not decisive, there has been a shift towards a unitary system. We have noted that the President appoints Provincial Governors. The latter can dismiss Provincial Ministers only with the President's concurrence. Conflicts between a Governor and a Provincial Assembly are resolved by the National Assembly. The ambit of central legislative power is now much wider and becomes all-embracing when the 'national interest' requires.

More important, the President appoints not only the Chief Justice but the judges of Provincial High Courts. The Courts can no longer decide whether legislation is *ultra vires*. Judges and former judges have been entrusted with high public responsibilities, and the Constitution ostensibly affords guarantees of judicial independence. But the President clearly intends not to be embarrassed by judicial review of the constitutionality of his policies. As we have stated, most of the fundamental freedoms of the Bill of Rights are now no longer justiciable.

Yet there are safeguards against dictatorship. Certain matters are excluded from executive influence, e.g. the administration of justice and the grounds for removal of a judge; the arrangement of electoral units and the supervision of the conduct of elections. The legislature is essential to certain acts of government, including, of course, the making of laws and the levying of taxes. The Speaker may summon the Assembly at any time at the request of one-third of its members. Whatever reservations must be made about this new form of government it would be difficult to argue yet that it offends sufficiently against 'Commonwealth principles' to justify exclusion—even assuming any such principles exist as a condition of membership.

Ghana is a more dubious case, though the position cannot be fully assessed until we have discussed later the general question of one-party states. When Ghana became independent in 1957 the constitution provided for responsible Cabinet government, a unicameral legislature elected by universal suffrage and safeguards for judicial and official independence. Certain rights were guaranteed and there was promise of a Bill of Rights (which never materialized). Regional assemblies were to be established as an alternative to the federal system which the Opposition had demanded, and certain bills for constitutional amendment would require the approval of two-thirds of these assemblies. All Bills to amend entrenched sections of the constitution required a two-thirds majority of Parliament. The Convention People's Party, however, already had such majority.

Within a few weeks the Constitution was amended, with the approval of the new regional assemblies, the elections to which had been boycotted by the Opposition, so as to dispense with all the special majorities and procedures required to amend the Constitution. The regional assemblies were then abolished, though they had in any case been given purely advisory functions. The functions of the regional houses of Chiefs were also reduced and matters concerning chieftaincies were placed under government control. The Judicial Service Commission was abolished and the Attorney-General compelled to follow the Prime Minister's directions with regard to prosecutions for offences against the State. The powers of the Public Service Commission were reduced.

Prescription of religious and tribal political bodies—to which Dr Nkrumah had always been unwilling to accord recognition as the official Opposition on the grounds that they were not national parties and not, constitutionally, 'alternative governments' (they had, in fact, used the device of the 'walk-out' from the legislature) —brought all the opposition elements together into the United Party. Preventive detention was legally possible even without a declaration of emergency and there was no independent tribunal of review. There was considerable interference with the judicial process and executive officers were indemnified by Act of the National Assembly for offences involving contempt of court. On the other hand, in 1959 an independent Commission found that the General Secretary of the Opposition Party and another Member of Parliament (though not Dr Busia and other prominent leaders) 'were engaged in a conspiracy to carry out at some future date in

Ghana an act for an unlawful purpose, revolutionary in character'. As Mr Gordon Walker has said, 'a government cannot ignore the sort of opposition with which it is actually faced'.

Meanwhile, the National Assembly was empowered to resolve itself into a Constituent Assembly. Government constitutional proposals were approved by it and submitted to a referendum. At the same time a presidential election was held. The Constituent Assembly then adopted the constitutional proposals with certain government amendments.

Although the Convention People's Party is nowhere explicitly mentioned in the new republican constitution it 'permeates the entire governmental structure'. The people are said to be the source of power, which, unless delegated under the constitution to particular institutions, is exercised by referendum. Certain parts of the constitution can be amended only in this way. Although the legislature must authorize taxation (though it cannot amend the annual estimates) and the raising of government loans, and the armed forces, it generally has a subordinate role. The President has plenary legislative powers except in respect of certain constitutional amendments. Bills are subject to his absolute discretionary veto which cannot be overruled. Cabinet ministers must be members of the Assembly but they are responsible only to the President. The latter may dissolve Parliament at any time (which also means a presidential election) but he himself cannot be removed.

The President dominates the constitution. Each general election is accompanied by a presidential election and is decided by the previously declared preferences of candidates for the National Assembly. The President appoints the judges and can remove the Chief Justice. This has, in fact, happened. He controls the civil service. There are, of course, certain limitations on his power besides those already indicated in relation to constitutional amendments and the powers of the legislature. He has no judicial power and superior judges and the Attorney-General are removable only by a two-thirds vote of the Assembly—though with a C.P.P. monopoly this is no obstacle. The President's solemn declaration on taking office affirms the principle of non-discrimination on grounds of sex, race, tribe, religion or political belief and also various basic freedoms—subject, however, to necessary 'restrictions imposed in the interests of public order, morality or health'. But these guarantees, of course, confer no justiciable right on anybody : they have not made void the Preventive Detention Act and other measures against political opponents.

There is no longer an independent non-political service. Trade unions and other 'voluntary' organizations are, in fact, organs of the C.P.P. of which the President is himself General Secretary. Special courts without jury and from which there is no appeal try offences against the State. In October, 1961, after widespread strikes, large numbers of strike leaders and opposition politicians (including Dr Danquah, for long the leader of the nationalist movement) were put under preventive detention—though very many of them were released after fifteen months.[1] The opposition newspaper has been censored. Ghana is now officially a one-party state. Many of these measures appear the more understandable in view of the obvious opposition even *within* the ruling party and attempts on the President's life involving some prominent party members. They may, indeed, be the only alternative to complete anarchy. Nevertheless they are clearly incompatible with the rule of law and within anything but a rather strange definition of democracy. Neither, as we shall see, may be possible in many African States. Indeed, as the *Economist* remarked on 9 January, 1965, it was 'not the African members who pioneered the road we have travelled along. In 1958 Ghana . . . was still a constitutional monarchy with a parliamentary opposition, at a time when Pakistan had already converted a republican system into a military government'. Nevertheless, the 'Commonwealth' as a whole can clearly do no more than 'seek to understand'. It cannot condone, at least as a permanency, without deserting every principle of its 'common ideals' or 'common political idiom'.

Tanganyika is our third and last detailed example of the presidential system within the Commonwealth. (There is nothing particularly distinctive about Kenya and Zambia except that the latter was the first to become independent *as* a Republic, while Cyprus is too *sui generis* to provide useful generalizations, and in any event, its constitution has broken down completely.) Against all expectation, Tanganyika was the first British East African territory to achieve independence—in December, 1961, nine

[1]Dr Danquah died in detention in 1965 of a heart attack.

114

months before Uganda and eighteen months before Kenya. The main reason for this speed in the stages before independence was a single-minded nationalist leader, Julius Nyerere, who was widely respected. Uganda, apart from the special problem of Buganda, was slower to develop national parties. Kenya had its white minority and tribalist divisions which for long prevented the emergence of one strong party, in the absence of a national leader, first through the imprisonment of Jomo Kenyatta, then by the reluctance of Britain until the very last to accept him as the inevitable leader of an independent Kenya. Tanganyika emerged to independence with a Westminster-type constitution, though not with one of its apparently essential under-pinnings, a two-party system. Most elections produced an overwhelming number of candidates who were returned unopposed. There was no basis for 'a significant interplay' between executive and legislature.

But the immediate cause of the replacement of the 1961 Constitution was the Government's desire to establish a Republic. One argument was that as a Trust Territory under United Nations supervision (originally a Mandated territory under the League of Nations after its removal from German control) Tanganyika had never been part of Her Majesty's dominions until Independence Day. People, it was further argued, could not understand the subtle distinction between a ceremonial Governor-General and the Government under the Prime Minister. The country needed an executive President. Proposals were approved by the National Assembly which then became a Constituent Assembly and then (without the royal assent) Acts were passed to provide for the new Constitution and the direct election of a President. Dr Nyerere was elected as President Designate by an overwhelming majority.

The President, unlike his counterpart in Ghana, has no direct legislative authority. Rights are specified in the Preamble to the Constitution, not in the Presidential declaration, but they are not justiciable. There is a Vice-President who is leader of Government Business in the National Assembly and to whom the President has delegated many of his functions. The President's legislative veto can be overridden within six months by a two-thirds vote of the Assembly. The latter, among other things, can reduce the estimates. It can amend the Constitution by a two-thirds majority at two stages.

115

The Chief Justice is not removable in the President's discretion and the office of a superior judge cannot be abolished unless vacant. There is an effective Judicial Service Commission, an Electoral Commission presided over by the Speaker and an advisory Civil Service Commission, though the principle of a politically neutral civil service has been abandoned. On the other hand, preventive detention is possible, though with procedural safeguards, and the Director of Public Prosecutions must comply with the President's directions. In 1962 politically appointed regional and area commissioners were appointed. President Nyerere's attitude has, perhaps hardened as a result of the army mutinies, and the problems posed by the union with Zanzibar (whose road to independence was far more stormy). But he remains in many ways a democrat at heart, sympathetic almost to the point of indecisiveness some might say, and, as Professor S.A. de Smith has suggested, 'at this stage only the intellectually blinkered would indulge in censorious reproof'.

VII: PARTY SYSTEMS IN COMMONWEALTH
COUNTRIES

In discussing Presidential systems we have touched upon the problem of one-party states. This phenomenon must now be examined more closely since more than any other, probably, it has engendered the feeling that Commonwealth members as a whole no longer possess any democratic ideals or practices in common. Neither the definition of a one-party state, nor the analysis of the factors which have led to its emergence is simple. The term is used of certain of the States in the United States where one party continues over a long period to win elections (which are, however, free except to the extent that in some places Negroes are still prevented from voting), and even to reduce the opposition to negligible proportions. It is even said that in some cases the few opposition members are elected on suffrance and must be acceptable to the majority party! Even at federal level there have been long periods of domination by one party (twenty-years for the Democrats from 1932 to 1952) although, of course, the opposition remains free, strong, and may even at times control one or both

Houses of Congress, which, with the separation of powers, poses problems for the strongest President. An American political scientist, during the period between 1951 and 1959 when it seemed possible that the Labour Party might never again win an election in Britain (it actually achieved an overall majority of only four in 1964), suggested the term 'one-and-a-half party system'! In India it is correct to speak of a 'one dominant-party system' at least at federal level but this is the result of honest victory in free elections. Indeed, there is no reason to believe that the virtual one-party state in Tanganyika emerged in any other way than by free election. As President Nyerere has suggested, you cannot artificially create an opposition if the socio-economic conditions for it do not exist.

Moreover, it must be admitted that one-party states may often be preferable (except in orthodox 'democratic theory') to such a splintered party system that stable government is virtually impossible. Ceylon's difficulties have arisen from factors other than the large number of parties or the tendency of large parties to split. Indeed those factors helped to *create* such a party system. But the difficulties might more easily have been dealt with had a more effective party system been possible. The British West Indies for long suffered from a proliferation of small parties in almost every island with the exception of Jamaica. On one occasion a Secretary of State for the Colonies refused to establish a Cabinet system with a Prime Minister on the grounds that it was impossible to foresee a firm party majority in the legislature. Nigeria's problem at the federal level has been the non-existence of national parties. The two alliances which fought the elections in 1964 were alliances of convenience (like that between the Northern People's Party and the National Council of Nigerian Citizens from 1960–1964). They seemed bound to break up after the elections, or to be unable to govern without including elements from the rival alliance (which, in fact, happened, though the precise details are too complicated to give here). Such a problem resulted from the fact that the Regions were virtually one-party and therefore a tripartite coalition seemed the only alternative to a feeling of isolation and unfair treatment on the part of the excluded Region. It was this which led to the events in the West in 1962 and the emergence of a breakaway 'Western' Party, the Nigerian National

Democratic Party, which could cooperate with the ruling alliance at federal level (though only at the cost of greatly handicapping its rival 'Western' party, the Action Group which many believed was more truly representative of the Region). Finally, as many acute observers of the African scene have emphasized, the alternative to a one-party system is often not a viable multi-party system but anarchy. It must be emphasized again that many opposition parties are regionally or tribally based and that they oppose not merely the majority party but the whole basis of the State. It is emphatically *not* true that rival parties would prefer to see the other side win rather than destroy the constitution (cf p. 82 above). Moreover, conditions in the 'emerging countries' are often held to resemble those of war-time in more developed states. Then, after all, it is argued, the cry is one of national unity and coalition governments, with the motives of opposition spokesmen questionable if not treasonable!

The further generalization must be made that our judgment may be affected by the *way* in which one-party regimes have come into being. In the first paragraph of this part we suggested certain 'natural' ways whereby this has come about. But there are other cases where every possible difficulty has been placed in the way of opposition parties by denying them access to the means of communication, by interfering with their electoral activities and eventually by detaining their leaders or forcing them into exile. Constituencies may be so arranged as to reduce or destroy the opposition (though 'gerrymandering' is not unknown in the western world!). Finally the State may be declared by law to be 'one-party'. The range of possibilities is all the way from a genuine feeling that the majority must be supported for the good of the country, through despondency at the unlikelihood of making an impression on the majority party, to the ultimate situation where opposition is rendered difficult, then impossible, then illegal. Those who can see no excuse whatever for one-party regimes and deny any possibility either of intra-party democracy or of what has been called 'tutelary democracy' in which the leaders honestly aim to maintain as much democracy as possible and to create the conditions in which it may eventually operate effectively, will, of course, condemn. We have quoted many opinions, however, and most recently that in *The Times* (above p. 76) that the

Commonwealth need not cease to exist, nor be despaired of because of these political deviations.

Examples of what, so far, we have referred to in general terms are taken from Africa. In 1962 the International Commission of Jurists stated that of nineteen tropical African States which had become independent since 1957 only four still had a significant Opposition party. Had Uganda and Madagascar been included in the list there would have been six—with Nigeria, Sierra Leone, Cameroon and Somalia. 'One cannot yet conclude', according to Professor S.A. de Smith, 'from the early experience of black African States that liberal democracy, as it is understood in Western and Northern Europe, North America or Australasia, is unworkable in Africa. The records of India shows that sweeping generalizations about the appropriateness of western political institutions for Asia may be incautious, despite the prevalence of authoritarian systems in that continent.' But there is a clear trend in Africa 'and there are good reasons for expecting it to continue in a large majority of the new states. Most of these States have regimes far more authoritarian than Pakistan's'.[1] Moreover, and this is significant, 'hardly any of those regimes have been imposed as a result of a manifest breakdown of a liberal democratic system'.

This is a book about the Commonwealth and we cannot devote much space to a consideration of French-speaking Africa. It is significant, however, that most of the States concerned learned what they thought were the lessons of the Fourth French Republic and as they became independent, provided for an executive President with a fixed tenure and eliminated ministerial responsibility to the legislature. At the same time there was the trend to one-party rule. After the first elections minority parties were represented in most legislatures. Within a year or two 'the Opposition was either in gaol or in the government; and to an increasing extent it is in the government!' There were varying degrees of authoritarianism despite these developments. 'Guinea is . . . perhaps to be placed in a class of its own; yet a visitor from Mali or from Ghana, would hardly feel ill at ease. And it was with Guinea and Mali that Ghana formed the loosely-knit (but ill-fated) Union of African States in 1960.'[2]

[1] *op. cit.* p.231.
[2] S.A. de Smith *op. cit.* p.233.

Britain and the Commonwealth

The inclusion of Ghana in this category brings us to the Commonwealth. It is true that developments in Ghana have sometimes been too gloomily assessed both by those who always expected that their inner doubts concerning the possibility of parliamentary democracy in Africa would be proved correct and by those who, perhaps over-idealistically, had such high hopes for the first African State to win its independence of colonial rule. But there has been a progression towards one-party rule which is certainly incompatible with what have generally been regarded as Commonwealth ideals and principles. The opposition was harried by threats, preventive orders, press censorship and many other forms of official discrimination. It may be true that opponents were dealt with less harshly than those in some of the other contemporary African States and that six years after independence there were still a few members of the National Assembly who did not belong to the C.P.P. But Ghana is now officially a one-party state. The slogan that 'Ghana is the C.P.P. and the C.P.P. is Ghana' has been legalized. Doubtless Dr Nkrumah had serious problems with the politically disruptive forces of tribalism and regionalism and the opposition certainly did not behave in a 'parliamentary' manner.

Convincing or otherwise, however, this explanation does not apply to Tanganyika (though it is more relevant to the problems created by the union with Zanzibar to form Tanzania). The Tanganyika African Union, once the colonial administration realized its strength and abandoned attempts to create a 'pro-administration' party on the pattern of French West Africa, never had an effective opposition to contend with and won every seat but one in the 1961 elections. Yet President Nyerere decided that recognition should no longer be accorded to the right to form opposition parties. He has attempted to justify his decision by persuasive constitutional and sociological arguments. Practical considerations doubtless reinforce these since the army mutinies and the involvement with the problems of Zanzibar. But the new constitution, adopted much more quickly as a substitute for the Westminster model than was the case in Ghana, is modelled closely on that of the latter state.

There are, of course, different degrees of *intra-party* 'democracy' in the various one-party states. Some discussions and disagreements take place in private; some may even occur publicly. President Nyerere claimed that members of the National Assembly would be able to criticize openly without being disciplined. In Malawi, however, dissident ministers and others were dismissed, threatened and forced to flee, while Dr Banda Hastings has the right to declare vacant the seat of any M.P. who deserts the party for which he was elected. In Ghana, there is a limit to intra-party disagreements; prominent members like the Finance Minister, Mr Gbedemah, have been compelled to go into hiding; on the other hand some members have been found guilty of conspiring against the President—not exactly an encouragement to tolerate opposition. Whatever may be the position about internal freedom to dissent, however, there is in the one-party state complete absence of the right of *organized* dissent and the right of the opposition to campaign for support as an alternative government. Nor is actual suppression always necessary. There is the control of public appointments, the siting of public works in particular areas and material benefits of every kind. The more responsible the Government becomes for economic and social development the stronger it is, so long as it meets with a sufficient degree of success not to endanger not merely itself but the regime (if the two can be thus separated). On the other hand, fear of failure may increase the necessity for control. We quote once more from Professor S.A. de Smith :

'In new African countries there exists a wide range of methods of clinging on to power, and a population that is well accustomed to receiving and complying with orders issued from above. One can hardly be shocked when advantage is taken of the opportunities thus proferred.'

Have not governments of 'advanced' countries been accused of distributing favours and manipulating budgets and economic development—even of withholding information—in order to win elections? And again,

'it is not altogether becoming for an Englishman to be shocked when the Government of a former British colony proceeds to apply for local political purposes the vigorous law of sedition that it has inherited, or to enact legislation along the lines of the Emergency Powers Order in Council with which it had been well acquainted in a different capacity during the colonial era.'[1]

It must be added also that the behaviour described above is not merely, perhaps not even primarily, to be ascribed to the self-interest of the rulers. There is the problem of building a nation and of developing a national consciousness, within boundaries artificially drawn by the colonial powers. Tribalism is a serious problem everywhere and not merely in the Congo where it has produced its worst consequences. Inter-tribal friction delayed independence in Uganda, and it is comforting rather than alarming that many members of the Kabaka Yekka party have abandoned Baganda particularism to join the Uganda National Congress in order to aid the creation of national unity, and that the Democratic Party, which rested to a large extent on a Catholic basis, appears to be in process of absorption. Yet Prime Minister Obote has, so far, steadfastly refused to listen to suggestions for the legalization of a one-party system. In Kenya, to the usual problems of an orthodox multi-racial society of Europeans and Africans there were added those of tribalism. The constitution under which Kenya achieved independence so firmly entrenched tribal regionalism that it made government almost unworkable. It is not, therefore, surprising that Ronald Ngala has led his KADU into President Kenyatta's KANU as a gesture, and an aid towards national unity. Kenya also affords an example of the problems of a tribalism which crosses the newly-established national frontiers, since the Somali of the Northern Province desire union with their fellows in Somalia across the border. We have seen that opposition parties often exist on a purely tribal basis. It is only necessary to recall the problems facing the British House of Commons during the period of the Irish Nationalist Party to realize how easy it is to bring the machinery of government to a standstill when the very legitimacy of the regime is in question.

Again, the economic and social problems of Africa differ not merely in degree but in kind from those which western governments have had to face—and there is now the 'example' of western

[1] *op. cit.* pp.235–236.

affluence which Africans wish to achieve in a tenth of the time which it took western countries. Strong government with a sense of urgency is required and it is argued that the burdens placed upon the people in the name of progress are no more than those imposed on a disfranchised working class by industrialists and landlords who virtually controlled a Parliament which for long refused to protect the voters. There is exaggeration—but some truth—in this. Illiteracy and ignorance have to be combatted *after* the achievement of universal suffrage and propaganda and over-simplification appears to be the only means of overcoming apathy or backward-looking opposition. It is argued also that able men cannot be wasted on the Opposition benches, and that, in any case, Africans do not understand the notion of an official Opposition which opposes the legitimate government. (Permanent and organized opposition to His Majesty's Government was frowned upon in eighteenth-century England!) Opposition is equated with disloyalty. 'Indeed, one has the impression,' says Professor de Smith, 'that the main single reason for abolishing opposition in parties is fear of the consequences of allowing an opposition freedom of action'—consequences not merely for the ruling party but for the nation.

VIII: THE FUTURE OF DEMOCRACY IN THE COMMONWEALTH

These general problems will be considered further in our section on the future of the Commonwealth. The *fact* of one-party systems is with us. Either they must be regarded as beyond the pale of a Commonwealth which cannot tolerate such deviations from its 'ideal type', or they must be accepted with as much tolerance and understanding as is demanded by 'free association' in a context of practical cooperation for whatever common ends continue to exist. In so far as common ideals of government and broadly common practices related to these ideals have been regarded as one of the 'links' of Commonwealth, they have largely ceased to exist except, perhaps as aims for the future. But the Commonwealth has not ceased to exist.

Mr Patrick Gordon Walker is one of the more optimistic prophets of the future. On Pakistan he wrote in 1960 that 'on balance it seems likely that Pakistan will in the end evolve its own variant of parliamentary democracy'. On Ghana :

> 'no explanations can escape the conclusion that parliamentary democracy in Ghana was in 1960 and 1961 distorted. But it was not destroyed. . . . Parliamentary democracy in Ghana was under strains that were not without parallel, but it was alive, had been embodied in a constitution and could be expected to survive, become stabilized and flourish.'

It is conceivable that these favourable assessments might have been modified if Mr Gordon Walker had been writing later. But the question still remains of the extent to which the Commonwealth depends for its survival on the maintenance in its members of a certain general kind of governmental system.

As Mr Gordon Walker, again, has written :

> 'A common stream of parliamentary democracy was the major source of the cohesion of the Commonwealth. It induced a capacity to cooperate and a habit of cooperation : it largely shaped the nature and machinery of Commonwealth consultation and the infrastructure of links of affinity that underlay the unity of the Commonwealth in action.'

But he goes on later :

> 'A failure or abandonment of parliamentary democracy would affect the nature of the Commonwealth : but it would not be fatal. A common parliamentary democracy was certainly essential to the coming into being of the Commonwealth : it created the fundamental political affinities between the members. But it is not indispensable to the continuity of the Commonwealth : the habit of cooperation that it brought forth could suffice to maintain a capacity to cooperate.'

What Mr Gordon Walker foresaw was

> 'an evolution and adaptation of parliamentary democracy

124

rather than its failure and abandonment. This would be a continuation of a process that is as old as the Commonwealth. In that case the challenge to the Commonwealth would be the ability of the members to keep in harmony their various developments of a type of democracy that is by its nature flexible and adaptable.'[1]

So much, then for the question of forms of government. Our next section turns to a whole group of factors which will determine the future of the Commonwealth and of which the 'common political idiom' may turn out to be only one, and perhaps not the most important.

[1]cf. generally, Patrick Gordon Walker, *The Commonwealth*, Part V. 'Prospects'

The Future of the Commonwealth

Consideration of the future of the Commonwealth has been implicit, sometimes explicit, in much of what has already been discussed in this book. Now, in this final section our aim is to attempt to draw together the suggestions which have been made in passing; to elaborate some of them in further detail and, finally, to attempt some general and very tentative assessment of future developments and prospects. This is being written at a time when official representatives of the Commonwealth are meeting in London to work out the details of the Commonwealth Secretariat which was proposed in 1964 and urgently pursued by the new British Government, and when the British Prime Minister has already begun to sound the Heads of other Commonwealth Governments about the possibility of another top-level Conference in the summer of 1965.[1] The precise significance of these developments may well appear more clearly even before this book is in print. If our attempt to foresee this significance is not entirely successful, this is a danger which all attempts at prophecy must risk. In any case we do not try to penetrate too far into the mists of the distant future. The changes in the nature of the Commonwealth and in the world environment in which it is developing will doubtless have repercussions on any subsequent changes and we do no more than try to see their immediate significance. Changes in the prospects for the entry of the United Kingdom into the European Economic Community or some kind of association with it; inter-

[1]This has now (Feb. 1965) been arranged.

126

national developments which may make more of a reality the Organization for African Unity or completely transform parts of the Commonwealth, for example in Asia where the effects of Chinese power are incalculable and the Malaysian-Indonesian conflict may bring either disaster or the merging of Malaysia with the Philippines and Indonesia to form the much discussed 'Maphilindo' Federation; changes in American policy which might, for example, by abandoning South Vietnam, open up a further threat to Malaysia and India which could destroy the Commonwealth in Asia—all these and many other factors are beyond our purview. In a sense our question is the very much simpler one : 'where will the Commonwealth be—and what will it be—this time next year?'

All the present signs are that the Commonwealth will certainly continue to be a 'going concern'. This is not a meaningless truism; there was ample room for fear that what earlier (p. 61) we described as the fourth great crisis in the history of the Empire-Commonwealth might, if not break it, cause cracks which could not for long be papered over. But the crisis was weathered only by laying the foundations of certain changes which will almost certainly have developed further in twelve months' time. Not long before the 1964 Conference a right-wing Conservative writing in *The Times* described the Commonwealth as 'a gigantic farce' and 'a disastrous encumbrance from which Britain must break free'. Just after the Conference a Cairo broadcast, presumably for the benefit of these African nations who had just played an important part in it and who were proceeding direct to a meeting of the Organization for African Unity, described the Commonwealth as 'outdated' and an organization that must be 'totally dismantled'. Yet not only did the Commonwealth survive the Southern Rhodesian crisis, as it had survived the South African crisis of 1961 and the tensions of 1962 arising out of Britain's application to join the European Economic Community; it appeared to emerge stronger than ever in many respects.

'You walk out only if you have nothing to say,' President Kenyatta of Kenya is reported as declaring : the African members had a great deal to say. What is more important is that what they said had considerable influence on British policy. And, it has been pertinently asked, how could they hope to exercise such effective influence without the existence of the Commonwealth? We have already suggested that no country remains within the Commonwealth after independence except for the reason that continued membership serves its self-interest. Although in the case of Britain history, tradition, sentiment and nostalgia are inevitably stronger than they are in other members—some of whom, however, also have such ties of 'affinity' to supplement their ties of 'interest'—she, too, derives considerable advantages of a practical kind from the maintenance of the Commonwealth. Were the views of the right-wing 'Conservative' already quoted to become general, it might, as the *Economist* remarked on 6 June, 1964, prove harder to bring the Commonwealth to an end than to maintain it.

> 'While it endures, any member who quits injures himself more than anyone else. If Britain were seriously to . . . set about winding the whole thing up, it might find the other members—African, Asian or whatever—so outraged that it would not dare to proceed in the face of the united hostility.'

Many, including the present British Government—and, indeed, probably the majority of 'Her Majesty's Opposition'—feel that there are also more positive reasons why the attempt should not be made.'

Indeed, these positive attitudes, as we have seen, were very much in evidence at the 1964 Conference. The carefully prepared practical proposals for further cooperation which were presented by Sir Alec Douglas Home, then British Prime Minister, were regarded with some misgivings, not because they would involve further machinery for the achievement of Commonwealth purposes but because they were felt not to go far enough. The demand for a Commonwealth Secretariat came from African and West Indian supporters—doubtless in part because of some dissatisfaction with the traditional role of the British Commonwealth Relations Office and with the customary British initiative in drawing up a proposed agenda which, on this occasion, involved an obvious attempt to relegate the Southern Rhodesian question to a place of relative unimportance. But the reaction to such dissatisfaction was a demand for *more* effective *Commonwealth* machinery, not a weakening of existing connections. There were further suggestions for a mechanism for the mediation and conciliation of disputes between Commonwealth members. Mr Margai, Prime Minister of Sierra Leone, even produced proposals for schemes of development finance on lines already used by the European Economic Community and frequently castigated by African States as a form of 'neo-colonialism'. All these things, as well as the general atmosphere of the Conference, revealed a general feeling that the Commonwealth was still important to all its members but also the feeling that it was high time to translate the 'equality of status' enshrined in the Balfour Declaration of 1926 into practice that conformed to it. This clearly meant a change in Britain's role in the Commonwealth. One basic aspect of this is well summarized in a letter to *The Times* (2 June, 1964) from Professor Silcock of the University of Malaya.

> 'The Commonwealth is no longer a wheel with only one centre of force and drive. If it is to survive at all, it will be as a lattice of increasing intercommunication and interaction. No monopoly of initiative and concern should be expected of the government, the people, or the press of the "mother country".'

One thing is certain. Any changes for the future will have to be based on an explicit recognition of what the Commonwealth now is and ought to be in the opinion of all its members. The transformation of the Commonwealth has taken place in such a way that even those who are concerned with political developments have not fully understood the significance of the process, or, in some cases, perhaps have not wanted to. So-called 'Right-wing' opinion in Britain, for example, which thrilled to Mr Churchill's refusal to preside over the dissolution of the British Empire, has to some extent managed to reconcile itself to the new Commonwealth with the thought that the newly-independent nations had accepted 'a sort of maternal British authority'. Even the new nations have sometimes hidden the realities from themselves or at least from others. When Mr Nehru rebutted his Indian critics who disliked their country's membership of a Commonwealth which included South Africa, he helped to shelve this problem virtually from 1949 to 1961 by emphasizing that membership 'ought not to be related to members' domestic policies'. But both 'British authority' and 'abstention from concern with domestic policies' are now revealed as myths. The realities which must replace them if the Commonwealth is to survive have yet to be clearly defined.

New organizations, new machinery and new relationships will have to be geared to the new tasks and above all to the possibilities of the Commonwealth. To these we now turn.

II : ECONOMIC RELATIONS IN THE COMMONWEALTH

On April 25–27, 1963, a Conference was held at Ditchley Park, Oxfordshire, on 'The Future of the Commonwealth'. Under that title an account of its deliberations was published in the same year by Her Majesty's Stationery Office. Although its sub-title is 'A British View', the document is a valuable account of the problems of the Commonwealth as seen by its members in all parts of the world. We have drawn very largely upon the papers prepared for this Conference, the discussions and reports of its Sub-Committees and the Summary of the Discussion in Plenary Session.

We deal first with the paper on 'The Economic relations of the Commonwealth' by Professor J.H.B. Tew of the University of Nottingham and the 'Report of the Economic Sub-Committee'.

From an economic point of view the Commonwealth countries are very diverse in climate and natural resources, human skills and standards of living. Such diversity presents the possibility of considerable gains from the development of intra-Commonwealth trade, whether it be in Australian grains, New Zealand meat and dairy products or Indian textiles. There is, of course, already a considerable trade in tropical foodstuffs and basic raw materials. About one-third of the United Kingdom's trade is with the Commonwealth and, taking all the other Commonwealth countries together, about one-third of their trade is within the Commonwealth. It is true, however, that from 1959 to 1964 the percentage of British imports coming from the Commonwealth has fallen from thirty-six per cent to thirty-two per cent, while the proportion of British exports going to Commonwealth countries has fallen still more sharply from thirty-six per cent to thirty per cent. Yet Commonwealth trade as a whole with the rest of the world has been rising and this despite the existence of preferential arrangements between Commonwealth countries. The Commonwealth can never be a self-sufficient economic unit, nor become a sort of *Zollverein*. But the full potential gain to be derived from expanding intra-Commonwealth trade is not being fully exploited, especially in the case of temperate foodstuffs, semi-manufactures and manufactures. On the other hand, to exploit this potential gain would be neither a painless nor a speedy process since it would involve changes in the economics of the developed countries and extensive economic development in the under-developed ones.

The argument is not for a Commonwealth 'Common Market' or 'Free Trade Area', as we remarked above. Most developing countries, for example, would continue to insist on some protection for their newly-established industries while Britain would clearly not completely abandon protection for her agriculture. Against this, however, it is clear that if world trade in general were made freer by a scaling down of tariffs, import and export quotas and subsidies, intra-Commonwealth trade itself would increase. The Commonwealth therefore has a common interest in fostering both intra-Commonwealth and world trade.

One practical consideration is of outstanding importance. Calculations as to future developments in intra-Commonwealth trade must rest upon certain assumptions about any future possibility of Britain's entry into the European Economic Community. (There are also political implications here, with which we deal later.) In view, however, of our opinion that the Commonwealth could not continue for long to exist in anything like its present form, if at all, if Britain 'went into Europe', we shall not pursue this aspect in detail. Suffice it is to say that whatever the conditions of entry, so far as trading and economic matters are concerned, the Conference discussions in 1962 made it clear that the Commonwealth must be affected economically by any likely terms for Britain's entry. Temperate foodstuffs, some tropical foodstuffs and materials and also some manufactured goods would certainly be affected.

So far as arrangements confined to the Commonwealth are concerned there is the further problem that under the Geneva Agreement on Trade and Tariffs (G.A.T.T.), apart from a very few reservations which Britain made on signing, any freeing of trade within the Commonwealth would either have to take the form of a common market or free trade area (which, as we have seen, is extremely unlikely) or it would have to be done on a non-discriminatory basis. This is not to deny the benefits of the latter, but it is not a means of creating closer economic unity between Commonwealth members.

We have already referred briefly to British agriculture. Home production is supported by subsidies and other means in such a way as to stimulate Britain's own high-cost production and thus to reduce the market in Britain for low-cost temperate foodstuffs and also for sugar cane. The problem of temperate foodstuffs might be tackled by international commodity agreements. One argument for these is that by raising world prices for such products they improve the standard of living in producing countries. But, conversely, such rise in prices harms the consumers of such products. Generally speaking, since farmers in the producing and exporting countries have a higher standard of living already than consumers in the importing countries, there might be no real gain. Agreements might, in theory, provide for the production of the commodity concerned to be concentrated in the regions of lowest cost; so far they have not and high-cost production has not been curtailed. The matter is too technical to pursue further, but in any case world agreements are not 'Commonwealth' agreements, though the Commonwealth might be in a postition to encourage and urge them and, as we have suggested, intra-Commonwealth trade would benefit by world improvements.

The problem of tropical foodstuffs and raw materials also affects many Commonwealth countries. International commodity agreements for such products is again a possibility and here the producers do have inferior living standards. The more the production of such goods in developing countries is encouraged, however, the less incentive is there for them to diversify their economies. The 'colonial' one-crop economy is likely to persist. Moreover, any proposal to encourage such lines of production, or even to pay too much attention to agriculture in general, as the West Indian economist, Professor Arthur Lewis, discovered when called in to advise the Government of Ghana, is likely to be stigmatized as 'ne-colonialism'. It is necessary, as the Socialist journal *Venture* suggested in September, 1964, for 'ex-imperial powers and newly independent countries to join together in discussing the meaning of neo-colonialism and ways to eradicate it.' But it may be a question of eradicating the *name* rather than certain measures which would be beneficial if only the psychological objection to them implied in the name could be eradicated.

With respect to manufactured goods, Britain's attitude to the Commonwealth is already very liberal so far as tariffs are concerned. But the British jute industry is protected from Commonwealth competition by other devices, and imports of textiles from India and Hong Kong are limited by bilateral agreements. There are also restrictions on manufactures from Pakistan and Malaysia. The probability is that British public opinion would not tolerate the abolition of these protective devices, still less accept an uncontrolled influx of further goods as other Commonwealth countries develop their low-cost manufactures. Such Commonwealth imports would most likely be looked upon with no more favour than cheap manufactures from, e.g. Japan. The majority of people in Britain, as we noted in our discussion on immigration, do not distinguish between 'Commonwealth' countries and other 'foreign' lands.

From the point of view of the Commonwealth countries themselves, many economists consider that they have given very indiscriminate protection to almost any local industry which can provide acceptable substitutes for imports. This attempt at a high degree of self-sufficiency, it is considered, is likely to lead to inefficient and high-cost production in the countries concerned. Yet unless overseas markets can be guaranteed these same countries are unlikely to concentrate on a few efficient manufacturing industries and to rely on more extensive interchanges of goods whether in international or in intra-Commonwealth trade. 'I can see,' writes Professor Trew, 'little prospect of economic growth in very many of the newly-independent Commonwealth countries except on the basis of the rapid development of the production of manufactured goods for export.' But such goods must be assured of a sale. It is noteworthy, however, that this kind of protectionism has long been pursued by the older dominions of Australia, New Zealand and Canada. It was their unwillingness to abandon their high tariff policies which made the results of the

Imperial Economic Conference at Ottawa as far back as 1932 so disappointing.

The extension of trade depends also on effective means of international payment. Many Commonwealth (and other) under-developed countries are often prevented from taking the imports required for development because, in the absence of counterbalancing exports they lack the foreign currency needed to pay for them. The Sterling Area (which, however, as we have seen is not coterminous with the Commonwealth, though an important factor in it) has assisted in alleviating this problem. Its future will depend very much on the services which Britain, as the banker, can continue to provide to the clients. But, if Commonwealth trade does not grow in line with world trade in general, many countries will seek to diversify their reserves and hold less sterling. The supply of sterling is also important from the point of view of the provision of capital whether by the issue of securities by Commonwealth countries to raise capital on the London market or by direct investment by the United Kingdom in Commonwealth countries. Any programme for more elaborate interconnections between Commonwealth countries must take into account the development of further capital investment. But if Britain is to expand her overseas investment in this way, her own balance of payments must be safeguarded. Remedies for these problems are not so much to be sought in Commonwealth as in international arrangements.

There are also many difficulties even in the apparently simple field of direct aid rather than expanded trade. In the long run, most economists would agree, aid must be judged by the extent to which it will provide the means for further development, especially in manufactures, rather than simply bolster up existing industries or contribute to the meeting of current expenses (though this is not to say that aid for projects which provide no *direct* return, such as schools, hospitals, roads, bridges, etc. cannot be justified). Moreover, attempts on the part of developing countries to lay down conditions about the use of aid, which may involve seeking assurances even about administrative efficiency and honesty, are again likely to be regarded as 'neo-colonialist'. The 'Commonwealth atmosphere' is probably the most conducive to the successful working out of *agreed* proposals which avoid such stigma.

In this way it has a considerable contribution to make to the solution of problems of the relations between developed and developing country, perhaps more than, for example, the Organization of American States which suffers from a suspicion on the part of Latin American countries with problems similar to those of Africa and Asia of 'yankee imperialism'. Nevertheless, from a practical point of view, the Commonwealth excludes an unduly high proportion of potential benefactors. While this may justify the channelling of most of Britain's aid to Commonwealth countries, thus strengthening Commonwealth links, it means, on the other hand that most schemes, like the Colombo Plan, will need assistance from outside the Commonwealth and particularly from the United States. This is the more so because of the need to extend long-term credit on better than ordinary commercial terms.

On the basis of these facts which have had to be stated in very general and over-simplified form, what Commonwealth developments seem likely to be beneficial and possible? It is clear that the nature of the economic links throughout the Commonwealth are extremely hard to identify and define and that there is room for difference of opinion about their importance both to the Commonwealth as a whole and to individual members. Since action on the part of Britain would still be most decisive we must remind ourselves particularly of Britain's protective attitude towards her own agriculture and the restrictions which she places on many imports from Commonwealth countries despite the fact that she also provides aid for the diversification of their economics which can only be achieved if markets are available. *Venture* in the issue referred to above (p. 132) faced up to this dilemma.

'Britain must take the lead among the affluent nations and look at the domestic economy with a view to making the adjustments necessary to ensure that our overseas aid programme is not negatived by protectionist trading policies. This kind of planning calls for courage, but industry should be induced to move away from producing the less sophisticated manufactures that the developing countries must sell if they are ever to emerge from poverty. At the same time Britain should make sure that she misses no opportunity to sell to the developing world the kind of goods (agricultural

135

and factory equipment and the rest) that its growing economies need.'

But how far would a government, however committed to such a policy in principle, be able to go, especially in conditions of economic crisis and complicated planning problems, concerned with 'backward regions' *at home*? The same, of course, applies to any increase of capital assistance. To look at the problem in this way does, it is true, appear to be 'Anglocentric'. But since the bulk of capital and technical assistance from within the Commonwealth must come from Britain, and since three-quarters of all intra-Commonwealth trade is conducted between Britain and other countries, her problems are at present the key to the whole question of Commonwealth economic relations.

We do not overlook our previous point that many Commonwealth problems can be effectively tackled only on the basis of world developments. Nevertheless, it has been suggested that the Commonwealth as a unit might be able to exert pressures through international organizations such as G.A.T.T. or the Organization for Economic Development and Cooperation (O.E.C.D.). Even this suggestion, however, has to take account of the probability that some Commonwealth countries might have more in common with some foreign countries than with some other Commonwealth countries; Asian and African members, for example, with the countries of Latin America. There is also the fact that some English-speaking African countries are already negotiating directly with the European Economic Community. In so far as these other connections reduce the possibility of effective *Commonwealth* action, it would appear, again, that Britain may have to attempt to continue to play a major role in international affairs for the benefit *of* rather than in close cooperation *with* her fellow Commonwealth members. An example of this would be the negotiating of world commodity agreements which clearly could not be confined to the Commonwealth. Another would be in any discussions concerning arrangements through the International Monetary Fund to enable countries which get into temporary balance of payments difficulties to draw an additional allocation of foreign currencies. Moreover, to encourage international actions of this sort would again avoid the danger of charges of 'neo-colonialism'.

The one field which seems most promising for real Commonwealth cooperation is that of technical assistance, the supply of experts and skilled personnel, advisers, training equipment, surveys and the provision of scientific advice as well as assistance of all kinds with education. Here the cultural, institutional and 'intangible' ties of Commonwealth make it peculiarly suitable as a piece of machinery to organize such assistance, and on a multi-lateral basis. At the 1964 conference the great majority of members showed a strong desire to make use of British methods despite any political differences. There is ample scope for all kinds of cooperative efforts, which are the more valuable because some of the economically poorer countries of the Commonwealth are none-the-less able to make significant contributions of 'know-how'. Among the projects which have been specifically mentioned in this connection are an Agricultural Cooperative Conference (along the lines of the Education Conferences which have been so successful) and the project for an institution for the training of senior administrators, both general and for development and planning, which is still (January,1965) under discussion in London. On these kinds of projects the Report of the Economic Sub-Committee of the Ditchley Conference concludes :

> 'To some extent the loss of an Empire has made British people uncertain where they belonged and where their mission in the world lay. The Commonwealth which is an association of widely differing States fully recognizes the obligation which exists between richer and poorer countries for mutual understanding and help, and it is to the advantage of everyone that this feeling should be exploited to the full.'

Some suggestions which were made in *Venture* (September, 1964) by Mr Harold Wilson, before he became Prime Minister, are very interesting in this context. First, he proposed a Commonwealth Exports Council.[1] There are already Government-backed councils for exports to Europe and the dollar area. Could there

[1]Several have since been established.

not be one for the Commonwealth? 'If one-tenth of the effort put into other areas had gone into a Commonwealth trade drive, our trade figures would be a lot better than they are today'. This is to emphasize the benefit to Britian; there is, however, no question but that Mr Wilson sees the development of intra-commonwealth trade as a means of strengthening the Commonwealth as a whole. Secondly, he proposed a Commonwealth Development Council. This would arrange regular meetings between the British and Commonwealth Governments to seek to coordinate development and capital investment programmes. Britain would also guarantee markets for the basic produce of Commonwealth countries and would plan her own industrial capacity on the basis of guaranteed outlets in the Commonwealth. The expanded functions of the new Ministry of Overseas Development mark a practical start to schemes of this sort. Finally, he proposed a Commonwealth Career Service. The idea behind this is to draw together the somewhat haphazard processes whereby posts are filled in developing countries and to work towards a pensionable career service for those who take up such posts. In particular, professional and technical experts who accept short-service appointments overseas would have their future safeguarded. The service, of course, would include such persons from every Commonwealth country with a contribution to make.

It is fair to add that in some respects these ideas were a development of the proposals made to the 1964 Conference by Sir Alec Douglas Home and elaborated still further under pressure from other Commonwealth representatives who, as we have seen, felt that they did not go far enough.

It is not easy to sum up this great variety of ideas, some seeking to build up on existing Commonwealth arrangements, some looking to more far-reaching new developments; some hard-headed and practical, some perhaps a little visionary in the light of existing hard realities; but all conscious of the fact that however significant the role of Britain may remain, *cooperative* efforts are the essential basis for future Commonwealth developments, and all realizing that the Commonwealth cannot become a self-sufficient economic unit, though it has a significant contribution to make to world economic development on which, conversely, its own future must depend. How *distinctive,* then, is the Commonwealth contribution likely to be? This cannot be answered on the basis of economic potential alone, and accordingly we turn to the political aspects.

III : THE FUTURE OF POLITICAL RELATIONSHIPS

The working paper for the Ditchley House Conference on 'The Political Relationships of the Commonwealth' was provided by Mr Dennis Austin of the Institute of Commonwealth Studies in London. Much of this paper deals with matters already discussed in other parts of this book. But it does also attempt to pick out certain specific problems which may affect future developments. The difficult nature of such an enterprise, particularly in view of the reasonable assumption that the future must to a large extent be governed by the implications of present tendencies is emphasized by the statement that 'the absence of any easily discernible growing points is still one of the most marked features of Commonwealth relationships. The only clear line of advance has been along a familiar path—towards an unfettered national sovereignty on the part of its members'.

Moreover, from the point of view of Britain, Commonwealth relations are not the only problem. There are also her relations with Europe and with the United States. Nor can Commonwealth relations be considered purely on the basis of historical connections, which do not have quite the same significance for all members. Further, even present day relations are not the same for all members. Those between Britain and the 'older Dominions', whether considered historically or as they exist today, are not the same as those between Britain and the newer members (though the differences are sometimes exaggerated, especially by those who are not altogether happy with the changes they profess to discern) and one may suspect that the most fruitful relations for the future are more likely to reflect the latter than the former.

Even if this were not true, the growing number of members must make those relationships somewhat different from those of the past. Meetings of twenty Heads of Government cannot be so intimate and informal as those between far fewer representatives, quite apart from any problems arising out of differing personalities and outlooks. The growing interest of newer members in matters hitherto reserved in practive very largely to British discretion may necessitate *more frequent* informal discussions, perhaps between just those members who are particularly interested in certain problems. They may even 'caucus' in private outside the Conference itself. But this interest will also mean larger plenary sessions at which, especially when controversial issues are raised, disagreements cannot necessarily be hidden from the public by vaguely worded communiques. We saw this in respect of Southern Rhodesia in 1964. For these reasons it is essential to look at some possible causes of friction which could in the future make the outward maintenance of apparent agreement somewhat difficult.

Sharp differences of opinion between Commonwealth members —as, for example, between India and Pakistan over Kashmir, Malawi and her neighbours over Pan-Africanism and relations with Portuguese Africa, Ghana and Nigeria over African affairs and international relations, Britain and some African members over the remaining problems of 'decolonization', to cite only a few possibilities—might affect Commonwealth relations in general. So far such differences have been resolved or shelved and have not affected general Commonwealth cooperation. But it may have been concern over possible future difficulties which made certain members put forward to the 1964 Conference tentative proposals for machinery for the conciliation and mediation of disputes. Conflicts between a member country and a foreign state—for example, between Malaysia and Indonesia or Ghana and her neighbours or Kenya and Somalia—might also strain Commonwealth loyalties. Some African members were a little reluctant to go too far publicly in support of Malaysia in 1964 because of the psychological appeal of 'neo-colonialism' from Indonesia and the desire for continued Afro-Asian cooperation in the United Nations. (Indonesia's withdrawal from the United Nations may perhaps, at least temporarily, have eased this problem.) Nor were all Commonwealth members equally perturbed at the worsening of Chinese-Indian relations, though in the long run this problem might weaken the appeal to some members of Communism.

How far is Commonwealth association compatible with widely

140

different foreign policies? What would be the effect of a unilateral declaration of independence by Southern Rhodesia and the possible establishment of a Government-in-exile and subsequent disturbance or even armed conflict? Would differences of attitude to this situation split the Commonwealth? What would be the effect of an uprising in South Africa? Or of more publicized and more elaborate attempts to overthrow Portuguese rule in Africa by armed force? It is easier to raise these questions than to attempt to answer them.

Although we have already argued that a common political philosophy is no longer a feature of Commonwealth links and, indeed, that one advantage of the Commonwealth may be its ability to hold together regimes of very different political outlooks, it is necessary to enquire how far such tolerance might be expected to go without the emergence of unbearable strains. South Africa was not acceptable for continuing membership because of strong objections to her policy of apartheid, and her application for continued membership as a Republic was used as the occasion to force her out. In 1964 it was clear that Southern Rhodesia under her present constitution was not regarded as a suitable member. It has sometimes been alleged that, apart from racial divisions between Negroes and East Indians, one reason for delay in granting British Guiana independence was the fear that a Communist, (or, at least, Castro-type) regime might be introduced. Perhaps only the cloak of respectability which was thrown around Zanzibar by her union with Tanganyika prevented the emergence of a question mark over her Commonwealth membership because of alleged Russian and Chinese (and East German) 'take-over' bids. Could the Commonwealth include a Communist or a Cuban-type member? We can only repeat that the best answer is Mr Austin's 'wait and see'.

Problems might also arise from the temporary nature of some of the boundaries of existing members. Some might break up. What, for example, would happen if three separate states emerged from the Nigerian Federation, possibly in a way which made friendly relations between them difficult? Or the breaking-up process might involve the relations between neighbouring African States (mutual recriminations about support for 'separatist' movements are not unknown); this might create difficulties between member states and endanger Commonwealth relations, although the India-Pakistan disagreement provides a precedent for hope.

More important, perhaps, is the possible creation of new units on a regional basis and the question of the retention or admission of such units. Some regional re-alignment might strengthen the Commonwealth; for example, the creation of an East African Federation of Kenya, Tanzania and Uganda. But suppose this were to include Somalia (which itself includes ex-British Somaliland and which is not a member of the Commonwealth), could it remain in membership? Or, if Ethiopia were also included? Could Malaysia remain a member if she joined with the Philippines and Indonesia? Or Ghana, if the future brought a more permanent union of, say, herself, Guinea and Mali. Would such units wish to remain members?

Again, some members, without being merged in such unions might become members of other organizations whose purposes were not compatible with those of the Commonwealth. Britain's position in N.A.T.O., where she is associated with Portugal, whose African policy is anathema to African States, is sometimes difficult. But other associations might pose more serious problems. We have already mentioned both the possibility that some English-speaking African States might joint the European Economic Community as Associate Members and the, perhaps somewhat more distant, possibility of a more effective and closely integrated Organization for African Unity. At the time of writing, Jamaica is considering a proposal that she should join the Organization of American States (with which she, like other Caribbean territories, shares many common problems). From one point of view these contacts might broaden the outlook of Commonwealth members and enhance the value of their contributions to Commonwealth discussions. From another, especially if exclusive economic links which adversely affected Commonwealth relations developed, the members concerned might come to regard the other organizations as more vital to their interests than the Commonwealth.

Enough has been said earlier on the possible repercussions of Britain's entry into the European Economic Community. Even if satisfactory conditions from an economic point of view were obtained so as to safeguard the interests of Commonwealth members, would the 'closer union', which the political implications in the Treaty of Rome involve, in the long run be compatible with the close association involved in Commonwealth membership, let alone with Britain's predominant role in it? To quote Mr Austin :

> 'Starting from a position of individual national sovereignty, the European countries are trying to move away from it : a reversal of the history of Commonwealth relations. United Kingdom membership might not affect (in the short run) its ties with the English-speaking member countries[1] since they are continually being reinforced (at present) by emigration from this country and they draw strength from a rich underlying sentiment of common origin. But full, active, continuing participation by Britain in the European Community would surely erode any special features of at least its official relations with the other Commonwealth countries'.

However, we may assume for the present that the formal ties between Commonwealth members will continue to exist; indeed, we have seen that they may be strengthened e.g., by the creation of a Commonwealth Secretariat. They will continue to provide for the communication of views between members on world problems and, in particular, a very special and intimate way for the communication of the views of the 'uncommitted' members who, apart from the United Nations itself, belong to no other groups and who are able to take different attitudes on world problems because they are not 'committed' in relation to cold war issues. The Political Sub-Committee of the Ditchley Conference thought that the political mistrust of some of Britain's policies might mean that 'the existing ties may be much weaker in ten year's time'. But this will depend to a large extent on the ability of other members to modify such British policies—as clearly did happen in 1964 over Southern Rhodesia. Even in defence matters and matters arising out of the cold war, differing viewpoints have not yet prevented close consultation and cooperation.

Further, the world situation could conceivably change in ways which might encourage rather than make more difficult closer

[1] i.e. presumably, the older 'Dominions'.

Commonwealth relations. The present disputes within the Communist world may lead to a less 'monolithic' confrontation of two incompatible ways of life. The understanding between some Communist countries seeking to loosen the bonds which bind them either to Moscow or to Pekin, and some Commonwealth 'uncommitted' countries may operate in this helpful way. In this context it is not impossible that assistance to African countries e.g., from Yugoslavia, Czechoslovakia and Poland might soften the acerbities of the cold war rather than mark its extension into another continent. (Though it would be difficult to sustain this thesis with regard to China.) On the other side, India's confrontation with the Chinese threat has tended to modify her 'neutralist' policy and to make her more aware of the significance of the Commonwealth to her. Similar changes of attitude towards Communism may develop from events in South-East Asia.

We have seen that from time to time differences appear between the old and the new members of the Commonwealth, particularly as regards what they hope to derive from its continued existence : on the one hand, the maintenance of a common belief in democracy, a sense of security, and the continued significance of ties of sentiment and blood; on the other hand aid, technical help, and a priority of assistance which might not otherwise be forthcoming. These differences, however, can be exaggerated. Both new and old members have links and interests outside the Commonwealth (Canada with the United States, for example). Both are determined to maintain their independence. Yet both —as seen, for example, in the attitude of Canada on the one hand and some African States on the other to the idea of a Commonwealth Secretariat—are anxious to develop those ties which are in their own interest. (It was Australia which was most dubious about the Secretariat.) Moreover, there are the growing links of interest between Australia and New Zealand on the one hand and Malaysia on the other; between Canada and the West Indies; between many members, new and old, and India in her struggle with China; between India and some of the countries of West Africa. Some of these links may have developed for reasons which lie *outside* Commonwealth relations, but in so far as they bring members other than Britain closer together they strengthen those relations. Moreover, both new and old members have cooperated in such peace-keeping activities as those in the Congo and although these are United Nations projects, collaboration between white and coloured even up to the level of top command is surely made easier because of Commonwealth membership.

Nevertheless it would be wrong to under-estimate the possible effect of differences of opinion, not merely between old and new members but between various groups of members, on fundamental issues. The future of the Commonwealth almost certainly lies pre-eminently in the future development of technical assistance, education, economic and cultural connections, both official and voluntary. So long as these continue to provide material and beneficial links, political differences are less likely to be pushed to the extreme where they might endanger other valuable forms of cooperation. There is ample scope for the increase of such forms of cooperation. We have already referred to some of the practical proposals which were made at the 1964 Conference and subsequently. Yet in some respects Britain is not as ambitious as, for example, France despite the failure of the latter to maintain the French Community. At the level of higher education British help to her ex-colonies bears more than favourable comparison with the French. Yet the latter continue to send some 7,000 teachers to ex-French West and Equatorial Africa while Britain sends less than 4,000 to *all* underdeveloped countries including some in Latin America. France has also appeared better able to foster the use of the French language in her ex-overseas territories than Britain has the use of English. Moreover, this is not just a question of basic English for practical purposes (though it has been said that there is a certain 'non-intercomprehensibility' between the various brands of English spoken). It is also a question of keeping before the eyes and minds of Commonwealth members, through their reading, the ideals which, however modified in practice at present, it is hoped they may eventually seek to achieve in their own countries. This might fruitfully combine with what has been described as the 'British example' (seen in action and not through any 'superior preaching') to influence future political development in many parts of the Commonwealth.

There are, however, certain things on which Britain clearly has to make a choice if this example it to be influential. One is, of

K   145

course the question of racial intolerance and discrimination. Here we must refer again to the Immigrants Act of 1962. However this may be explained it was clearly the result of increased immigration of West Indians, Africans, Indians and Pakistani and of the expression of colour prejudice. Although the Act applies equally to all Commonwealth citizens, the clauses demanding that immigrants should have means of financial support, a job to go to, or certain labour skills, are far more likely to exclude coloured immigrants in practice than Canadians or Australians. The argument that Britain has merely brought her laws into line with those of other Commonwealth members merely emphasizes the fact that Canada's immigration policy has for long excluded Asians or other coloured people (with some relaxations in 1962) and that Australia pursues a 'White Australia policy'. It may also be cited in support of any discrimination imposed by African States in East and Central Africa against Indians. Even the present Labour Government has felt constrained to continue the Act until agreed means of controlling immigration have been found, though there is a proposal to make certain acts of racial discrimination, so far as existing minorities are concerned, illegal by Act of Parliament. As has been said,

> 'In the Commonwealth eighty-five per cent of the people are Asian or African; but British power and influence are the most important cohesive elements and if it is to become a truly multi-racial society, then Britain must make an effort to re-educate her people in the ways of tolerance commensurate with the leading position she holds'[1]

Another issue is that of maintaining a sense of responsibility for bridging the gap between the advanced and the underdeveloped nations, with which is also involved the question of the best way to prevent the spread of Communism. Here economic sacrifices may be necessary on the part of the advanced nations.

Both racial issues and economic issues may, of course, have repercussions in the field of foreign and defence policies, especially as regards attitudes towards the cold war.

Let us return to the point that there may be certain differ-

[1]Guy Arnold, *Towards Peace and a Multi-racial Commonwealth*, p.145.

ences of attitude between the old and new members of the Commonwealth. If these differences are related to the key issues described above then the way in which they must be resolved so far as British policy is concerned cannot be in doubt. We quote again from the Political Sub-Committee's Report :

'We in Britain really do have to make a choice between the bonds which have been built up from here, based on race, and the new but genuine association which has been emerging with new nations. If the realities of why we should stick to the Commonwealth concept are accepted, even at the price of distortions in British policy and of distractions from our own Atlantic problems of partnership and defence; if, that is to say, we recognize the fundamental importance of the two broad struggles going on in the world, those of the cold war and the moral issue of help to the under-developed nations : then we must choose to act in the sphere of the new Commonwealth rather than the old. This is Britain's choice and it must be made now'.

This was written in 1963, after the 'expulsion' of South Africa, which seemed to indicate that such advice was already in mind, and before 1964, when it was surely followed, particularly in relation to the problem of Southern Rhodesia.

But certain tests are still to come. The issue of Southern Rhodesia itself is by no means yet resolved. There may be questions raised in the United Nations, when unless Britain is to be divided from her African fellow-members, she will have to speak out more openly and behave less legalistically than for long was the case when the problem of apartheid in South Africa was raised, or the latter's attitude with regard to South-West Africa. We have already mentioned the possible situation in which there might be an African Government-in-exile opposed to a Southern Rhodesia Government which had declared unilateral independence. This book does not seek to advocate particular policies, but it is permissible to point out that support for such a Government as the former would certainly be expressed by African members of the Commonwealth and expected of Britain by them.

Nor is the issue of South Africa completely resolved by the

147

fact that she has left the Commonwealth. We mentioned the controversial question of the role of sanctions as a means of bringing to an end the policy of apartheid. The present British Government is supporting the United Nations action in relation to an embargo of arms but the question of economic sanctions remains. Were Britain to attempt to remain neutral in any struggle over Southern Africa it is doubtful whether her relations with African Commonwealth members could remain satisfactory. There is also the further problem of how to end Portuguese colonial control of Angola and Mozambique without producing irreconcilable divergencies of opinion within the Commonwealth. These issues are not unconnected with the problem of the cold war since some argue that any support for conflict in Africa arising out of them might fail to solve the problem, but only open up the Continent to more Russian and Chinese Communist influence. This issue might again lead to further differences of opinion within the Commonwealth. On the other hand, the more optimistic assessment is 'that if countries like India did not leave the Commonwealth over Suez, they would not necessarily leave over South Africa or Southern Rhodesia'.

SECTION FOUR

Conclusion

In this last section we attempt to place the Commonwealth in the setting of world problems and to ask again what contribution it may have to make towards their solution. As throughout the book, much of what we have to say will be concerned with Britain's role in the Commonwealth, though this can be divorced neither from her attitude towards the other members nor from their attitudes towards Britain. We explained that our title was intended to indicate our primary concern with *Britain* and the Commonwealth. If in this section our emphasis is again on this we do not imply that Britain has either the ability or even the desire to impose her own will or to seek uniformity. But we must again assert that the future of the Commonwealth may well depend most vitally on Britain's actions and attitudes, both positive and negative.

Let us first indicate what have been described, in different words by different writers, though all in general agreement, as the five great challenges of the age in which we live. They are the scientific and technological revolution; the ideological struggle between communism and democracy, the problems arising from the break-up of the great European-dominated Empires, the issue of racial relations especially between coloured and white; and the great gulf between living standards in rich and poor nations. Each of these is important to Commonwealth relations and to the future role of the Commonwealth in the world. They are in many ways inter-connected.

Technological and scientific changes have been the main factors in creating rapid economic advance in certain nations of the world. This economic advance has helped to widen the gap

149

between the richer and the poorer nations. This division is almost the same as that between the coloured and white nations. The coloured nations form the bulk of those areas which are no longer parts of Empires and which are facing the problems which emerge when independence is achieved. Finally, the basic appeal of Communism is to the coloured, economically backward nations of the world, struggling to throw off what they regard as the last vestiges of imperialism and finding, in many cases, that democracy is an ineffective system for rapid modernization.

All these problems face the Commonwealth, as a microcosm of the world as a whole. Apart from Britain and the older Dominions, members suffer degrees of poverty which mark the immense disparity between the 'haves' and the 'have-nots' among the nations. This is in large part due to the fact that these poorer members have not yet received the advantage to be derived from the scientific and technological revolutions which, so far, have merely enabled the imperial power to conquer and exploit the rest. We need not emphasize the extent to which racial problems are the key to Commonwealth relations, but only point out that the ability of educated leaders to work together in the Commonwealth regardless of race does not yet mean that all the *peoples* of the Commonwealth, least of all those in Britain and the older Dominions are without racial prejudice. Communism is of concern to the Commonwealth partly because India, for example, lies in the path of its most likely line of expansion in the form of Chinese aggression; partly because in under-developed areas it provides a superficial attraction especially in relation to rapid progress. Every member has some contribution to make to the solution of these problems. But let us restate the case for believing that Britain's role will be decisive, and this time in the words of Mr Guy Arnold in his book *Towards Peace and a Multiracial Commonwealth* :—

> 'Britain is the centre of the Commonwealth and its future will depend on what she does. Nearly all the binding forces that cement the Commonwealth association together have their origin in Britain; the common traditions of government, law and custom; the people of immigrant stock who regard Britain as 'home'; the bulk of the trade and the main

source of the investment capital and aid; the greatest
military power; in short, all the keys to Commonwealth
unity are in the hands of Britain; without her the Commonwealth would fall apart.'

We have already suggested that some of these 'binding forces' are
wearing somewhat thin and that some of them (like 'immigrant
stock') are largely irrelevant so far as the majority of Commonwealth members are concerned. But we agree with Mr Arnold
that :—

'This is neither to say that the other members do not have
great responsibilities, nor that they are subordinate to
Britain. The principle of equality is the very essence of the
Commonwealth. But even an association of equals will not
function properly without a leader and for the time being
this can only be Britain. Eventually', he goes on, 'the leadership may well be taken by India for one day she will undoubtedly be by far its strongest member'.

It is not necessary to agree with this last specific point in order to
emphasize that leadership will almost certainly be shared, and
perhaps one day taken over, by some member other than Britain.
    What then, in general terms, should be the objects of leader-
ship? Mr Arnold suggests four, and we would find it difficult to
better his description of them. First, the members of the Commonwealth must constantly strive to achieve a real sense of understanding among themselves. Secondly, a target of a basic minimum standard of living must be set for the Commonwealth as a
whole so that the vast majority of its members can be enabled to
abolish their extremes of poverty and backwardness and reach
the 'take-off' point into economic modernization and social progress. Herein lies the peculiar responsibilities of the richer countries, Britain, Canada, Australia, and New Zealand; though, as
we have seen, outside help will certainly be necessary. Thirdly, a
truly multi-racial society must be created so that all 'Commonwealth citizens', irrespective of race, colour or creed will learn to
accept each other. If this non-racial community is ever to be
achieved there are no more likely places for its birth and growth

than the Commonwealth. Finally, and we have referred to this before, the Commonwealth must aim to assist in breaking down the gap which exists between the Western and the Communist world, for without this, all other problems will remain unsolved.

These are far-reaching objectives and the reader must attempt to judge from the account given of the present Commonwealth and its potentialities whether they are likely to be achieved. The greatest difficulties may well arise less from the attitudes of leaders than from those of the public opinion to which they so often feel it necessary to defer. Speeches which may be critical of the policies of fellow members may be delivered 'for home consumption'. They are taken with the necessary 'pinch of salt' by those who appreciate the sometimes devious ways of politics. But the relatively uninformed to whom they are delivered at home or similar people abroad to whom they may be reported in either garbled or exaggerated form, may take such speeches too seriously. The 'Commonwealth atmosphere' is thus polluted at the very point where it most needs to be freshened. For it must never be overlooked, in the words of the Ditchley Conference Report that :

'. . . the Commonwealth is an association of peoples rather than an organization of Governments. While there is much that Governments can and should do, the real strength of the partnership lies in the ties of friendship that bind its peoples together. In the modern world of easy travel, the degree of personal contact between individuals in every walk of life, throughout all Commonwealth countries, is increasing rapidly; this personal contact and understanding can be fruitfully extended by action on the practical lines (discussed above); in all these, if advantage can be taken of the opportunities, lies hope for the future'.

As the Duke of Devonshire, then Minister of State for Commonwealth Relations, told a large audience from some thirteen bodies that compose the Joint Commonwealth Societies, as well as representatives of many organizations and offices concerned with Commonwealth affairs, which had assembled for a two-day conference on 'The Commonwealth in Principle and Practice' on 16 and 17 October, 1963 :—

Conclusion

'If I was asked to say, 'what is the Commonwealth?' I would say, ' "Here it is in this hall this morning" ' He went on to say what a vital role all of the voluntary societies were playing. 'They are the essence'.

But again, whether we speak of governments or of voluntary bodies, the passing of the Anglo-centric Commonwealth is inevitable. As Mr Patrick Gordon Walker concludes his book :

'The Commonwealth will complete its fulfilment and maximize the cooperation of its members for its inherent moral ends when it becomes in truth and without inhibition a Euro-Afro-Asian Commonwealth . . . Time is on the side of such a Commonwealth as this'.

Some foreign observers may perhaps recall Alexis de Tocqueville's famous aphorism, 'the British Constitution, it does not exist'. Some equally exact political scientist might be tempted to say the same of the Commonwealth. Yet both have continued to exist, to grow, and to change; the first in the pragmatic manner of which the British are supposed to be masters; the second with a shared pragmatism practised by every member of the Commonwealth, though sustained by a vision without which it would long since have perished.

INDEX

155

Index

Index

For Product Safety Concerns and Information please contact our EU
representative GPSR@taylorandfrancis.com
Taylor & Francis Verlag GmbH, Kaufingerstraße 24, 80331 München, Germany